Making Your Place a Home

By Kevin Ruedisueli

quick fox

New York   London

ACKNOWLEDGMENTS

Special thanks go to Jan Wampler, and to Mickey Bliss for many things.

Thanks also to: Paul Alimi, David Bliss, Jack Chesley, Wei Chiu, Dixie Clark, The Cleveland-Marshall Community School, Kathy Drew, Tom Dreyer, Nick Elton, Diana Esterly, Francis Fleetwood, Bob Fritzsche, Kathy Futornick, Candy Gianetti, Todd Hamilton, George Hauser, Jack Howell, Bev Kelley, Lance Laver, Corrine McCarty, Marian Moffet, Craig Rafferty, Bonnie Richter, Martin Silfen, Margie & Peter Stern, Madeline Sullivan, James Taul Jr., Judy Uhl, George Weiner, Jeff Weiss, and Patty Weser.

International Standard Book Number: 0-8256-3068-1
Library of Congress Catalog Card Number: 76-56574
Printed in the United States of America.

In Great Britain: Book Sales Ltd., 78 Newman Street, London W1, England.
In Canada: Gage Trade Publishing, P. O. Box 5000, 164 Commander Blvd., Agincourt, Ontario M1S 3C7.

Designed by BPS Books, Inc.
Cover design by Iris Weinstein
Illustrations by Kevin Ruedisueli
Photographs by Herbert Wise and Kevin Ruedisueli
We gratefully acknowledge Jan Wampler, from whose home many of the pictures in the Photo Section were taken.

CONTENTS

PREFACE

Within all of us lives the image of the house of the soul. The housing of that which is truly us. An echo of ourselves, the dreaming, thinking, fantasizing, changing the place where we rest, love, eat, laugh and cry. The leaving of our imprint on an object or place for people not yet born to see and feel. It is the process of making — the making of echoes.

Yet, that which is within us has become hard to express. The art of making has become remote — often lost. It is difficult to get started or even know where to start. That which was obvious to generations past has become blurred, making it a difficult task just to know where to begin. We need all the help possible to start.

This book is about getting started — about a beginning. It is not a pattern book, although it has plans to build objects and places. Perhaps starting with a plan will lead to more. The first shelf may lead to a table, to a room, or to a house, each with the imprint of the maker. The act of housing the soul is ever continuous, ever adding, and ever changing.

This morning, I made a cabinet using mostly castoff material found on the street. I built without a plan but with ideas that grew upon ideas. As the materials were measured, cut, and fastened together, the cabinet became a house of the soul. The soul, arm, hand, tool, and material became one. An imprint of myself. I will continue tomorrow, learning from the mistakes of today. I was getting started — starting to make.

Jan Wampler

Jan Wampler, noted author of *All Their Own*, Professor of Architecture at MIT, creator and experimentor with old things, is my friend, my teacher, my mentor. — Kevin Ruedisueli

INTRODUCTION

It's a book for people who like to make things for themselves and their homes, who like experimenting with different ideas, who don't have much money, who like exploring rubble, who appreciate the beauty in an old thing, who like to use their hands, who don't mind dirty hands.

It's about useful self expression, and *not* about principles of decoration. It's a catalogue of project ideas with directions: ideas that use old or salvaged materials; ideas that are alternatives; ideas I've seen, heard-of, built, and invented; ideas for houses or apartments, and for public places within apartment buildings; ideas for individuals and for groups of individuals. It's about using what you have on hand, or can find in the street. It's about learning to build for your place and for others who will live there later. It's about walls that you can use, windows that are eyes, doors that are places, places that are homes.

There are eight chapters of ideas followed by an appendix that has anything else you need to know. You'll find information on tools, tool kits for the projects, materials, building procedures, ways and places to find supplies — especially used building materials.

Nearly anyone can learn to build the projects in this book. Some projects take practice, others don't. Building skillfully is an art which requires desire, patience, and the willingness to make mistakes. Beginning and the fear of making those mistakes are often the greatest barriers to cross. Knowing that you *will* make mistakes makes them less horrible. In time, beginning will be easier and mistakes fewer.

This book is meant to help people begin.

ABBREVIATIONS USED IN THIS BOOK

l.f. = linear feet
 ' = feet
 '' = inches
no. = number
 d = penny
s.f. = square feet

Making Your Place a Home

Wood Stud Wall

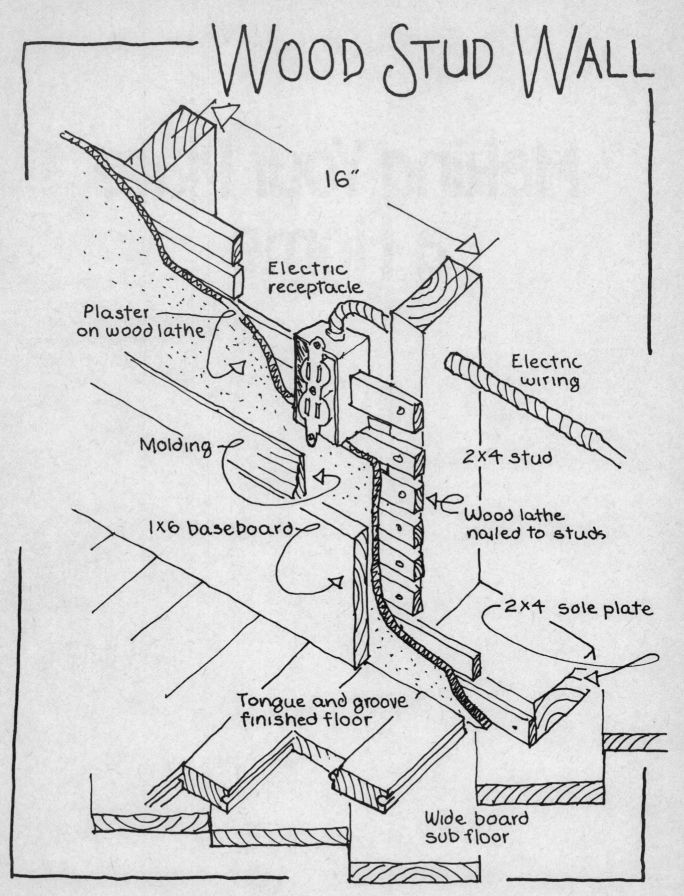

16"

Electric receptacle

Plaster on wood lathe

Electric wiring

2x4 stud

Molding

Wood lathe nailed to studs

1x6 baseboard

2x4 sole plate

Tongue and groove finished floor

Wide board sub floor

2

WALLS

The ideas in this chapter range from the creation of simple wall hangings, to cutting openings in walls, to actually building room dividers or functioning wall surfaces.

The first drawing is of traditional interior wall construction. Contemporary methods have substituted either metal lathe and plaster, or plaster board (also called gypsum board, sheet rock, and drywall) for wood lathe and plaster. Apartment buildings and dormitories may have walls that are concrete block, metal studs with plaster, or solid plaster. All walls are either partition or load-bearing. Partition and load-bearing walls often look alike. Partition walls, however, serve no structural function, while load-bearing walls support that which is above them.

If you are going to attach anything weighing more than a few pounds to a wall, you will need to know (1) what the wall is, and (2) how to attach to it. If the wall has wood studs, you can locate them by knocking, or with a stud finder, or by driving test nails into inconspicuous places. Studs will normally be 16 inches from center to center. Old houses often have studs on 12-inch centers. The measurement should be true except near corners or around openings, where spacing breaks down. If the wall is concrete block, brick, or solid plaster, use expansion shields (p. 174). If the wall has metal studs (it will sound like a drum when you tap on it), use Molly bolts (p. 174).

Magnet suspended in plastic case responds to presence of nails driven through plaster-board or lathe into studs

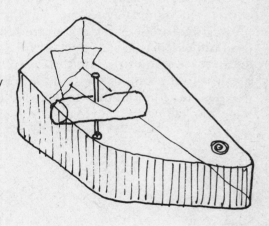

STUD FINDER

FABRIC ON THE WALL

The easiest and least expensive way to cover a large section of wall is to staple a patterned sheet to it. Even a cheap stapler will do the job. It is most easily done by two people, one to stand back and check for level, the other to use the stapler. The staples will do very little harm to the sheet or wall (less harm than tacks or tape), and they remove easily. For neatness of appearance, plan ahead and space staples at regular intervals.

You can also hang heavier fabrics, such as quilts, rugs, tapestries, but you may not want — nor be able — to staple through them. There are several methods for hanging heavy materials. You can buy plastic clips that stick to the wall. You may prefer to sew a wood strip into the top of the fabric and nail or screw it to the wall, or sew loops into the fabric.

Beware of fabrics that stretch, and remember that the sun can cause fading.

Skill Level: Simple

Tools: Stapler or First Kit

Materials: Patterned sheet, quilt, or other fabric; staples, plastic clips, sewn loops, or strip of wood plus two-inch screws

FABRIC ON THE WALL

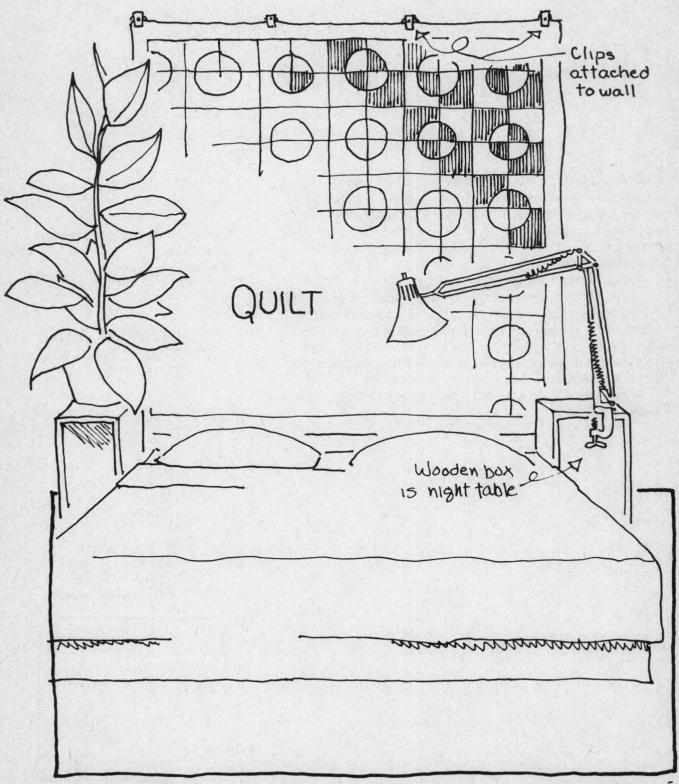

Clips attached to wall

QUILT

Wooden box is night table

STRETCHED FABRIC PANELS

Wood stretcher strips for canvas are sold at art supply stores. But you don't have to stretch canvas on them. Colored or printed fabric is OK too. Silk, acetate, cotton, burlap — all will work. Like stapled fabric, this can cover a large portion of wall. But you can use smaller pieces of fabric, and you won't have to sew any long straight seams.

To use stretcher strips:

1) Assemble the interlocking strips by hand — corners tight.

2) Starting in the middle and working on opposing sides, stretch fabric across the edge and tack or staple to the sides or back.

3) Hammer the supplied wedges into the inside corners to further tighten your fabric.

Six carefully aligned 1- to 1½-inch nails will support the six panels in the drawing.

Skill Level: Simple

Tools: Hammer
Staple gun (optional)

See also: Stretched Fabric Window Screen, p. 42.

Materials: Fabric
4 stretcher strips per desired panel
Upholstery tacks

INTERLOCKING STRETCHER STRIP CORNER

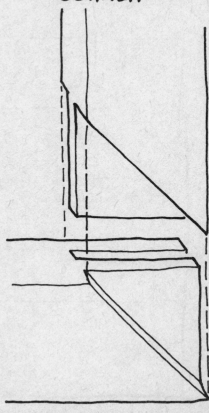

STRETCHED FABRIC PANELS

FABRIC PANELS
USING ARTIST'S
STRETCHER STRIPS

Mattress Couch

TACK WALL

This idea uses an inexpensive material called homasote. It has a quality similar to that of thick cardboard, and you can get it at a lumber yard. Homasote comes in 4- by 8-foot sheets with varying thicknesses. It is very durable as a tackboard, especially when properly mounted, and its appearance is greatly improved either by painting with a latex paint or covering it with fabric like canvas or burlap (burlap fades). It is possible to buy homasote that is prepainted white.

One way to attach fabric to it is with staples. First cut the homasote to a desired size. Then place it on the fabric and wrap the fabric around the edges, stapling it to the back of the homasote.

The drawing shows 2 1/3 sheets of homasote attached to a standard plaster wall. The joints between sheets of homasote are vertical and left exposed. To prevent buckling, the homasote should be nailed or screwed at 16-inch intervals (28 nails or screws per 4x8 sheet). Try to drive nails or screws into the wall studs.

If the wall doesn't have wood studs, attach 1- by 3-inch strips every 16 inches. Use Molly bolts or expansion shields to hold these firring strips to the wall (two or three will be enough for each strip). Nail the homasote to the firring strips.

Skill Level: Basic

Tools: Basic

See Also: Molly Bolts and Expansion Shields, p. 174.
Wood Stud Wall, p. 3.
Peg and Shelf Rail, p. 10.

Materials: Three 4x8 sheets homasote
1 lb. annular ring nails or
1 box (100) 1½" no. 6 round-head screws
8¼ yards of 54-inch canvas
10' of baseboard (see sketch)
10' of peg and shelf rail

TACK WALL

Peg & shelf rail covering top of homasote in same manner as baseboard–(see also page 10)

Kids art work, posters, etc.

Pattern or instructions tacked-up for convenience.

TACK WALL IN WORK-PLAY ROOM

Design painted directly onto homasote

Baseboard protects homasote from feet

work table

CROSS SECTION OF BASEBOARD DETAIL

10d finishing nail

½" Homasote behind baseboard

Existing plaster wall

1x4, 1x6, or 1x8 Baseboard

Peg and Shelf Rail

The Shakers, widely known for their furniture making, like to hang everything not in use on the wall — even chairs! They did this easily and neatly by running a strip of wood, with pegs at close intervals, five or six feet above the floor around every room. The result is a molding that divides the wall into two sections, and suggests ways of combining decoration and utility. For example, the top and bottom portions of the wall can be painted different colors, or the lower portion could be made into a tack wall.

The addition of a shelf to the top of the wood strip provides a place for small clutter items like photographs, postcards, and vases. Coats, hats, sweaters, umbrellas, and even a bicycle may hang below.

To build it, use no. 2 pine or some salvaged molding. Drill the holes for the pegs first. Be careful to maintain a consistent angle of the drill and equal distance between holes, as slight variations will show. Use a carpenter's level to draw a horizontal line on the wall. Attach the peg strip to the wall with 8d finishing nails driven into the wall studs at an angle such as you would hang a picture. Position the nails about ¾ inch from the top edge of the strip rather than in the middle. If your wall does not have wood studs, use Molly bolts.

Skill Level: Basic

Tools: Basic, back saw, and mitre box

See Also: Molly Bolts, p. 174. Tack Wall, p. 8.

Materials for 8 feet of rail:
16 ft. 1x4 no. 2 pine
8 ft. corner molding
3 ft. 3/4" dowel
Wood glue
1/4 lb. 8d finishing nails

PEG AND SHELF RAIL

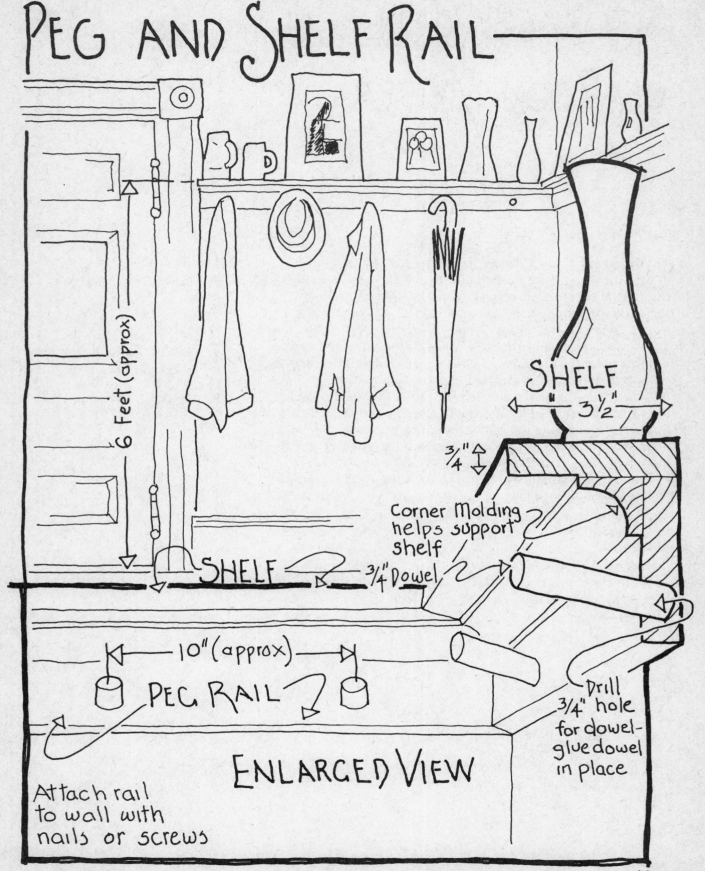

6 Feet (approx)

SHELF

SHELF
3½"

¾"

Corner Molding
helps support
shelf

¾" Dowel

10" (approx)

PEG RAIL

Drill
¾" hole
for dowel-
glue dowel
in place

ENLARGED VIEW

Attach rail
to wall with
nails or screws

11

Storage Wall or Room Divider

This storage-wall room divider is constructed of 1- by 2-inch, 1- by 3-inch, and 1- by 12-inch pine boards. It is made so that the vertical supports are connected to the floor and ceiling. The shelves are free to be removed or added to.

To construct the vertical supports, position the 1x2s on the 1x3s and clamp them with "C" clamps temporarily while you drill the holes for the bolts. The bolts are ¼-inch diameter stove bolts of various lengths, depending upon the situation.

The mounting plates that go next to the floor and ceiling limit the number of bolts into the floor and ceiling to a minimum. Six lag bolts will hold the ceiling mounting plate and four will hold the floor plate. The vertical supports then connect to the mounting plates with 2½-inch wood screws.

Note that if you intend to use plastic tubs, their dimensions will be useful during planning.

Skill Level: Basic

Tools: Basic and two 3-inch "C" clamps

Materials:
- 45 l.f. 1x2
- 64 l.f. 1x3
- 27 l.f. 1x12
- 16 l.f. 2x12, or 32 l.f. 2x4
- 22 1/4x1-3/4" stove bolts
- 30 1/4x2-1/2" stove bolts
- 10 3/8x2-1/2" lag bolts
- 16 2-1/2 no. 8 wood screws

STORAGE WALL

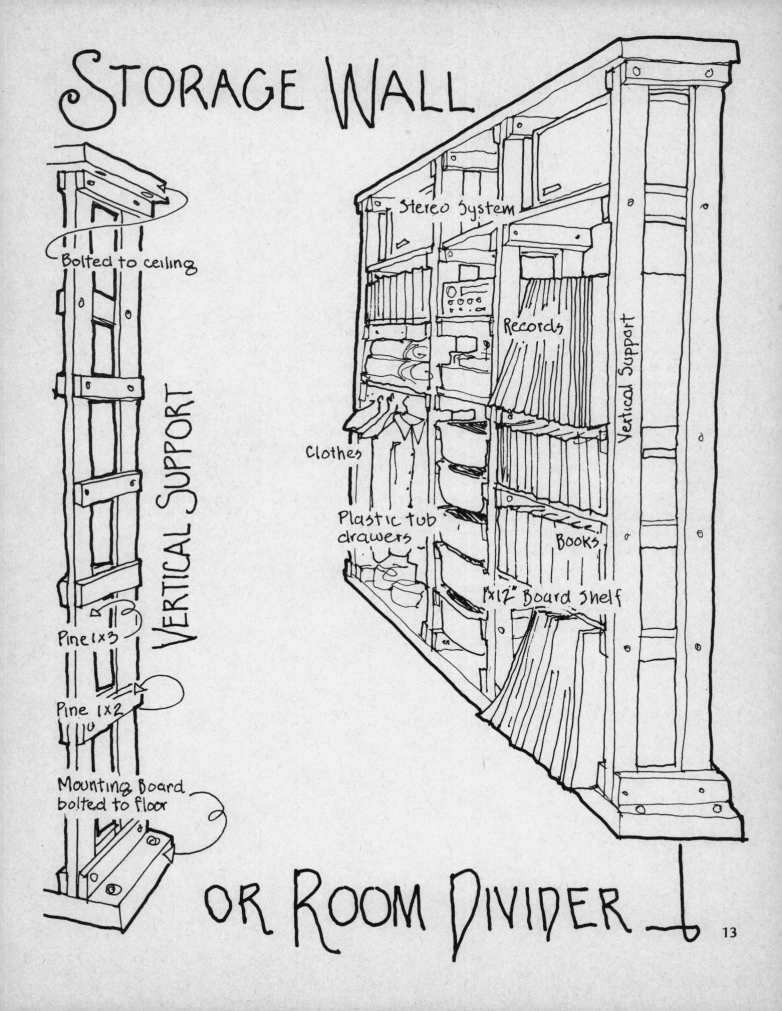

Bolted to ceiling

VERTICAL SUPPORT

Pine 1x3

Pine 1x2

Mounting Board bolted to floor

Stereo System

Records

Vertical Support

Clothes

Plastic tub drawers

Books

1x12" Board Shelf

OR ROOM DIVIDER

Adjustable Wall Shelves

These shelves are an improved version of a set which I built for myself. The major components are four steel angles screwed to the wall, shelves of various widths, and brackets (made of the shelving materials or of plywood) that bolt to the steel angles. I reclaimed the angles from some old utility storage shelves which were bent and useless, but the standards needed only repainting.

Screw the standards to wall studs, giving spans of about 32 inches for shelves. Cut the brackets out and drill holes for bolts, matching the holes in the standard. To avoid unnecessary remeasuring for hole locations, use one bracket as a template for the others.

Adjust spacing between shelves to suit your needs. Nine inches is about right for most books, twelve inches for oversized books.

These shelves would also provide useful storage space in a kitchen or workshop. (*See* p. 165)

Skill Level: Basic

Tools: Measure
Square
Saw
Drill
Screwdriver
Surform tool for smothing cut edges
of brackets.

Materials:
4 steel angle standards
12 2" no. 10 round-head screws and
washers
6 1" x 8" x 8' boards
4 1" x 12" x 8' boards
20 ¼ x 1¼" stove bolts and nuts
20 ¼ x 2" stove bolts and nuts
80 ¼" washers

ADJUSTABLE WALL SHELVES

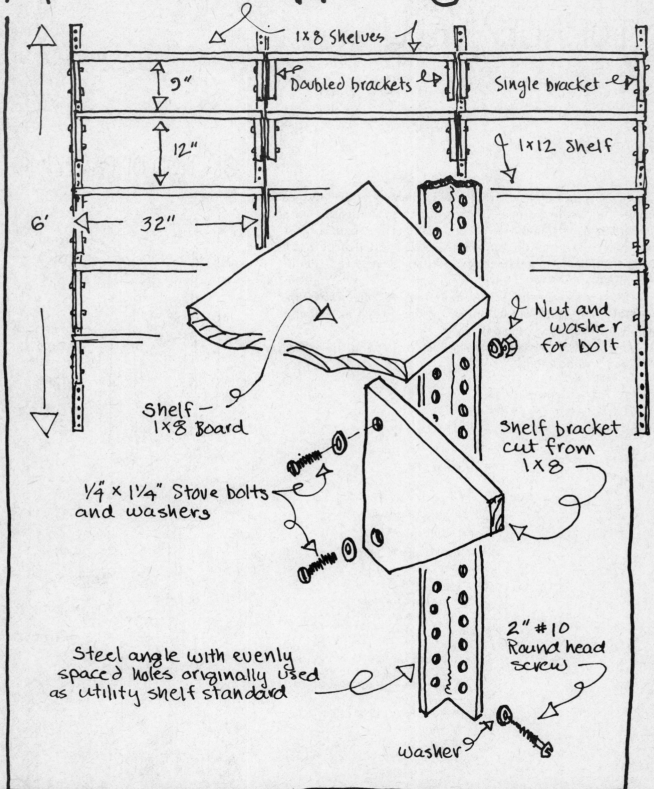

1x8 Shelves

Doubled brackets

Single bracket

9"

12"

1x12 Shelf

6'

32"

Nut and washer for bolt

Shelf — 1x8 Board

¼" x 1¼" Stove bolts and washers

Shelf bracket cut from 1x8

Steel angle with evenly spaced holes originally used as utility shelf standard

2" #10 Round head screw

Washer

Built-In
Storage Wall

The construction in this drawing relies heavily upon salvaged materials. Old-fashioned paneling, when cut into individual or small clusters of panels, makes excellent doors. These panels often have mortise and tenon joints and are well-suited structurally to be doors. They are inexpensive, and their quality is difficult to reproduce.

Drawers are another salvageable item. A collection of matching drawers from an old laboratory, store, or school will appear meant for their new purpose.

The panels and drawers are collected first and the cabinetry designed around them.

Skill Level: Advanced

Tools: Cabinetry

See Also: Hanging Doors, p. 176.
Drawer Glides, p. 132.

Materials:
Panel sections for doors
2 hinges for each door
Old door or desk top
Drawers
1x12 boards for uprights and shelves
3 lbs. 8d finishing nails
1x2s for framing around doors,
    drawers, etc.
3/4" plywood for desk pedestal and
    small doors
Hooks, pegs, or knobs for coats
Glass, wood, brass or porcelain knobs
    for drawers and doors.

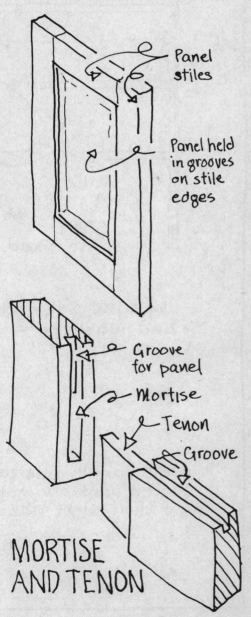

SECTION OF PANELING

Panel stiles

Panel held in grooves on stile edges

Groove for panel

Mortise

Tenon

Groove

MORTISE AND TENON

BUILT-IN STORAGE WALL

Doors cut from salvaged panels

Storage for
iron and
sewing supplies

Desk top made from a door

Fold-out
Ironing board

Step ladder
to reach
high storage

Salvaged drawers

HOLE-IN-THE-WALL WINDOW

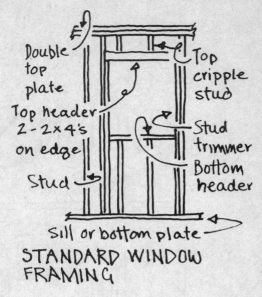

STANDARD WINDOW FRAMING

Double top plate
Top header 2 - 2 x 4's on edge
Stud
Top cripple stud
Stud trimmer
Bottom header
Sill or bottom plate

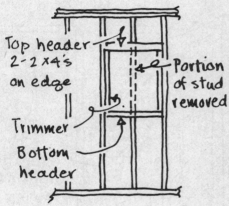

Top header 2 - 2 x 4's on edge
Trimmer
Bottom header
Portion of stud removed

Adding a window in an entrance area, or opening part of a wall between two rooms, is a good way to establish visual connection between spaces — a kitchen and a living room, for instance. The easiest way to make an opening is to cut out part of the wall between two studs. The structure of the wall will not be disturbed. However, this simple approach will limit the width of the actual opening to about 13 inches, if the studs are 16 inches from center to center. To attain a wider opening, it's possible to cut through one stud without worrying about the house collapsing around you, providing you then support that "crippled" stud with a header as shown in the small sketch.

A sabre saw is a good tool for cutting a plasterboard or wood-lathe and plaster wall. It will cut quickly but won't make too much dust, and the blade is easily replaced if it becomes dull or broken. You can use a hand saw, such as a compass or larger cross-cut saw if that's what you have, but the plaster will dull the blade.

Locate the studs and mark the desired opening with a pencil. Be sure the lines are vertical and horizontal. Watch out for wiring that may be in the wall. (*Don't* make the hole above or below a switch, for instance.) A good way to start the cut is to drill a hole or a series of holes that will allow you to insert the saw blade. Clean up the mess as you go along. Plaster dust has a way of tracking itself all over the house.

Make a box out of 1x6s 1/8 inch smaller than the opening you've cut. Slide it into the opening and nail it to the studs with 8d finishing nails. Patch the plaster around the edges with *patching plaster* — not spackle. Unless you want glass or a door in the opening, all you need to do is finish the 1x6 frame. Glass should be 1/8 inch smaller than the opening it is to fit. Hold it in place with moldings or 1x1s nailed to the frame as shown.

Skill Level: Basic (advanced if you hang a door in the opening)

Tools:
Measure
Square
Saw
Sabre saw
Electric drill
1/2'' chisel and mallet for hanging the door

See Also: Hanging a Door, p. 176.
Elaborate Entry, p. 38.

Materials:
1x6s for the frame
1x1s to hold the glass
Section of panel for the door
8d finishing nails
1-1/4'' or 1-1/2'' brads for nailing the 1x1s

HOLE-IN-THE-WALL WINDOW

HOLE CUT BETWEEN WALL STUDS
FRAMED WITH 1X6 BOARDS

Clear, colored, leaded, or no glass at all

Inside of wall

1X6 frame nailed to 2X4 studs

Door made from salvaged paneling

1X1's nailed to 1X6's

2X4 Stud

Glass

CUT-AWAY VIEW

Glass or brass knob

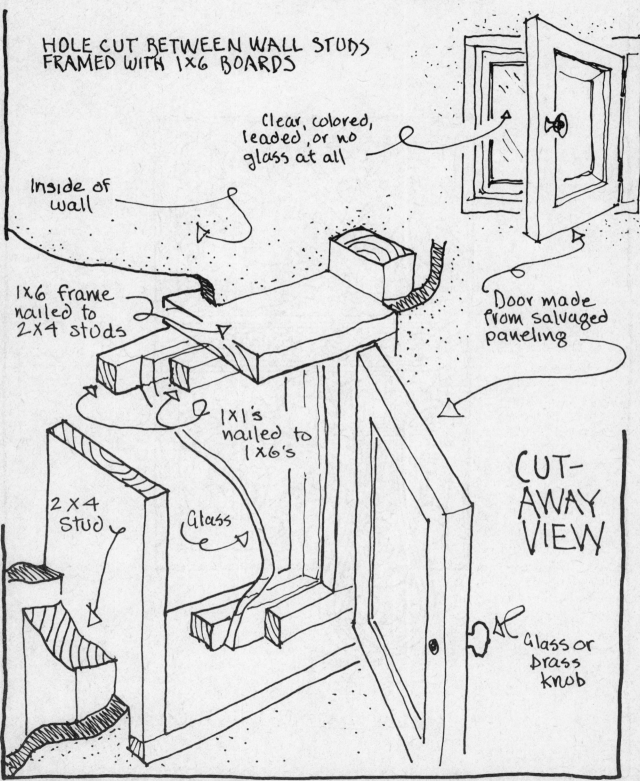

AN OLD GATE LOCK

From <u>Beautiful Houses</u> By Louis H. Gibson, 1895

Doors

Your door may be the first part of your world that an outsider sees, and it expresses something about you whether you actively assist it or not. A bare door has its message, as does an entire building of bare doors.

Doors are entrances to private worlds within worlds — a child's bedroom within a family's apartment within a tower. Some innovative people painted a sunflower and initialed their door. They built a place around their door to see themselves in a mirror, to show themselves, to hang coats, leave muddy shoes, messages, wait and explore for a moment; they created a functioning place.

Door Decoration

These sketches apply in particular to apartments or homes where there are flat "flush" doors, especially metal ones. In apartment buildings, doors from apartments to corridors must conform to a "fire rating," so it is rarely possible to replace them with ones that are more individual. But you can decorate them. To paint a metal door, prepare the surface by sanding the gloss from the present finish. Repaint it with exterior enamel paint. Prime bare metal with primer meant for the purpose. Masking tape can be applied to get straight, clean edges.

Skills: Simple to advanced

Tools: None, except for hanging the door

See Also: Hanging a Door, p. 176.

Materials:

To paint:
Sandpaper
Brushes
Enamel paint
Thinner
Masking tape
Newspaper or dropcloth

To make collage:
Collage materials
Thumb tacks, household glue, or tape

To replace a door:
A door the same size or slightly larger than the existing door.

Door Decoration

Poe

Name or design painted on a door

Collage glued, tacked, taped, or otherwise attached to door.

Old "panel" door replaces interior "flush" door

Hall Tree

A hall tree or rack is a piece of furniture designed expressly for entrance halls. Since few places now have entrance halls, it has become obsolete.

While these pieces sell for $200 or more as antiques, it is still possible for an alert person to find one cast aside in an attic, garage, cellar or town dump.

Another idea is to make an assemblage of articles that would combine to serve the same function as the hall tree. Substitute a trunk or box for the seat. Hang a mirror and/or a shelf on the wall. Attach a few brass coat hooks or doorknobs.

See also: Doorknob Coat Hooks, p. 30.
On the Wall Near Door, p. 32.

HALL TREE

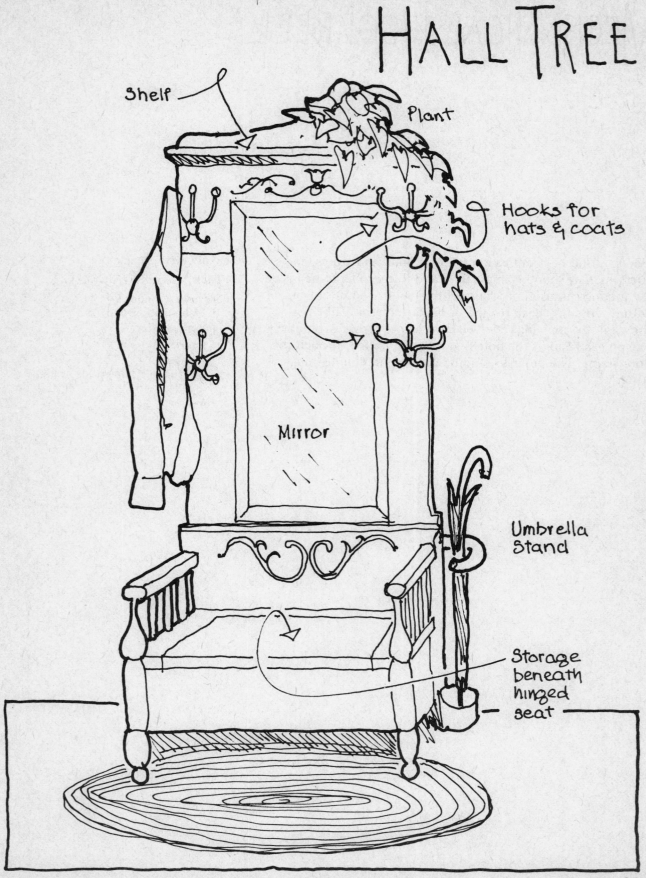

Shelf

Plant

Hooks for hats & coats

Mirror

Umbrella Stand

Storage beneath hinged seat

MECHANICAL DOORBELL

You can find bells in flea markets, second hand stores, and at auctions. The sound is important, and if it's going to be inside, the loudness is also important. If the bell has no mechanism with it, you may need to find or make something like that shown in the drawing. The bell cord passes across two pulleys, one on each end of the hole that must be drilled through the door frame. The pulleys could be the type in double-hung windows.

Skill Level: Simple

Tools: First Kit and drill

See also: Windows, p. 41.
Elaborate Entry, p. 38.

Materials:
Bell
4' rope
Bell bracket, homemade or found
2 pulleys
6 screws

MECHANICAL DOORBELL

Bell rope seen from outside

Bell rope to outside

Pulley and bell bracket screwed to wall

BELL MECHANISM

Small bell with a pleasing sound

Mailboxes

A mailbox can be nearly anything that is of an appropriate size and will contain the mail. The three shown here range from simply hanging a basket, to altering a box of the right size to suit the need, to constructing one from scratch. If you have energy but lack the skill to make your own, the second alternative may be the best. Here the slot and name tag are opportunities for self-expression. (*See* p. 164)

Skill Level: Ranges from none to advanced

Tools: Range from First Kit to Cabinetry

See also: Hanging Doors, p. 176. Swing-Down Drawer, p. 130.

MAILBOXES

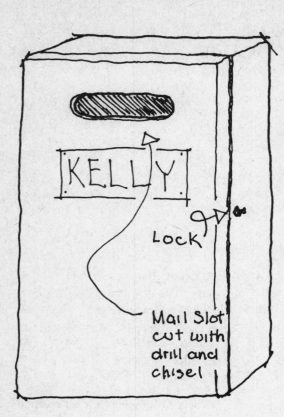

HINGED BOX

From a Flea Market

KELLY

Lock

Mail Slot cut with drill and chisel

WICKER BICYCLE BASKET

HANDMADE OAK MAILBOX

Old letter slot

LETTERS

BLISS

9"

Lock

Dowel for hinge

Name plate

Viewing holes

Doorknob Coat Hooks

This project is not difficult. The hardest steps will be cutting the board to mount the knob on, and mounting that board to the wall. A round shape complements that of the doorknob, but isn't absolutely necessary.

You can cut a round shape with a sabre saw. (A cardboard template will keep the mounting boards consistent in size.) A vise or some method of holding the board will help while you are cutting and smoothing it.

Smooth the edges with a Surform tool and sandpaper. Drill a 3/8-inch hole in the center for the dowel. Cut the dowel to an appropriate length and file it square on one end to fit into the doorknob. The set screw of the doorknob will hold it on. Glue the dowel into the hole in the board.

Mounting the board on the wall may be a little tricky. It will have a tendency to split when nails are driven through it, so drill pilot holes just slightly smaller than the nails. Position it over a stud and nail it to the wall. If you wall doesn't have wood studs, use Molly bolts or expansion shields.

The mirror is useful on the way out of the house. You might locate one mirror at adults' eye level and one at kids' eye level. (*See* p. 162)

Skill Level: Basic

Tools: Basic Kit plus sabre saw and pocket size Surform

See also: Appendix, Molly Bolts and Expansion Shields, p. 174.

Materials:
Collection of doorknobs
3/8" x 3' dowel
3 or 4 8d finishing nails per coathook
2 round mirrors
Wood glue and/or epoxy cement

Doorknob Coat Hooks

KNOBS NEATLY
ARRANGED
ON A WALL

Mirror from
army surplus
store

Wood cut to
desired shape
attached to wall
with 8d finishing nails

Coats on knobs —
low knobs for
short people

Hole
for dowel

Set screw

3/8" Dowel
filed to fit
into doorknob

Ornate
doorknob

METHOD OF MOUNTING
DOORKNOB

ON THE WALL NEAR DOOR

This is a way of making a functional collage on the wall. As drawn, it serves the entrance area with places to hang coats, leave messages, or check yourself in the mirror before leaving. The homasote and painting will in time fatigue and need replacing. The box could be any wooden box with dimensions that serve your desired purpose; nail wood dividers into it with wire brads. Old desk seats will be either rare or bountiful. These items appear in salvage and junk yards when outdated school buildings are demolished. They are made of cast iron (may be rusty — but repairable) and are great as plant stands.

Skill Level: Simple

Tools: First Kit, except for doorknob hooks

See also: Tack Wall, p. 8.
Doorknob Coat Hooks, p. 30.

Materials:
Small piece of homasote
Old mirror or picture frame
Pictures
Door knobs or hooks
Mirrors
Old school-desk seat

ON THE WALL NEAR DOOR

Painted homasote message board & painting in old picture or mirror frame

new photo in old frame.

round mirror

Coat on old door-knob — see page 30

notes

Mirror for Kids

Long, narrow box with dividers added — pigeon holes for mail, envelopes, stamps, pens, note pad, tacks. . .

Old school desk seat – plant stand.

Shelf Coat Rack

This is similar to the peg and shelf rail, except the shelf is wider and must be supported by shelf brackets. Here the shelf brackets are cut out of the same material as the shelf and backboard.

Skill Level: Basic

Tools: Basic Kit

See also: Peg and Shelf Rail, p. 10.
Doorknob Coat Hooks, p. 30.

Materials:
 1x8 no. 2 common pine
 1/4 lb. 6d finishing nails
 Doorknobs and 3/8" dowels, *or*
 Coathooks, *or*
 3/4" dowel

SHELF

Hats on shelf

WELCOME

Doorknobs, hooks, or dowels

8"

EXPLODED VIEW

8d finishing nails

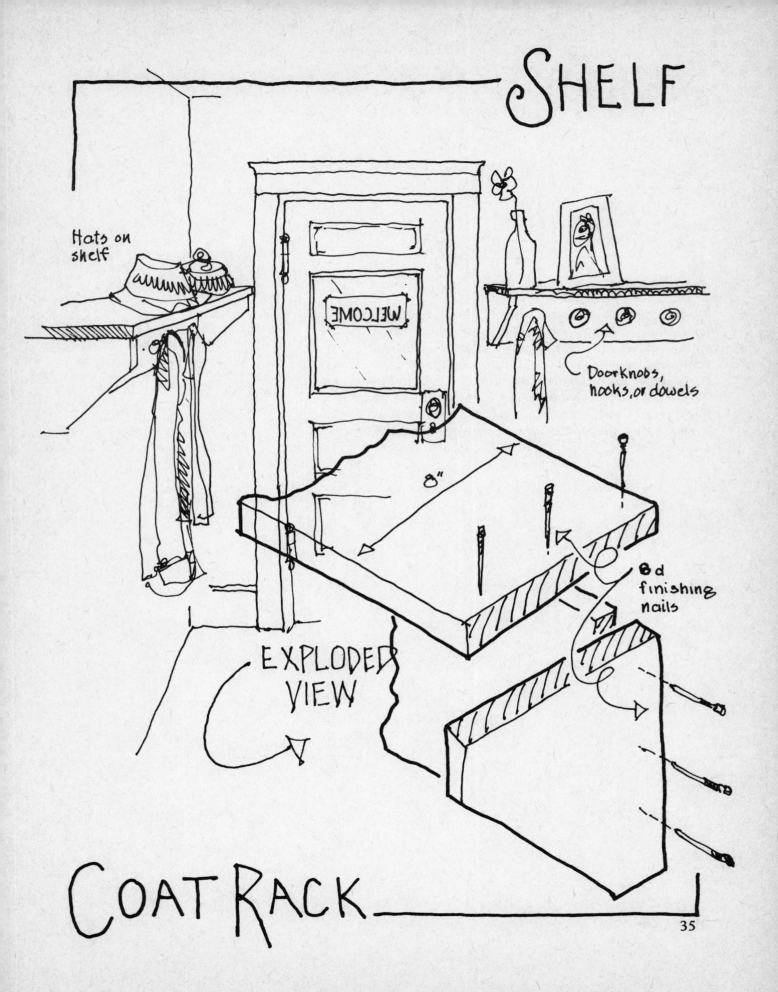

COAT RACK

STAIR ENTRANCE

This is a common entrance to apartments in two- and three-family houses. A stair goes past each apartment. Though not within your apartment, the landing is on your turf and is yours to treat as you will. You could work with the other people in the house to paint and decorate the entire hall, and you could put special things on your landing to show that it's yours. You might choose a hall tree or seat, peg and shelf rail, coat hooks, a mirror, a picture, a plant, a welcome sign. . . . anything that in some way is you.

See also: Hall Tree, p. 24.
Peg and Shelf Rail, p. 10.
On the Wall Near Door, p. 32.

STAIR ENTRANCE

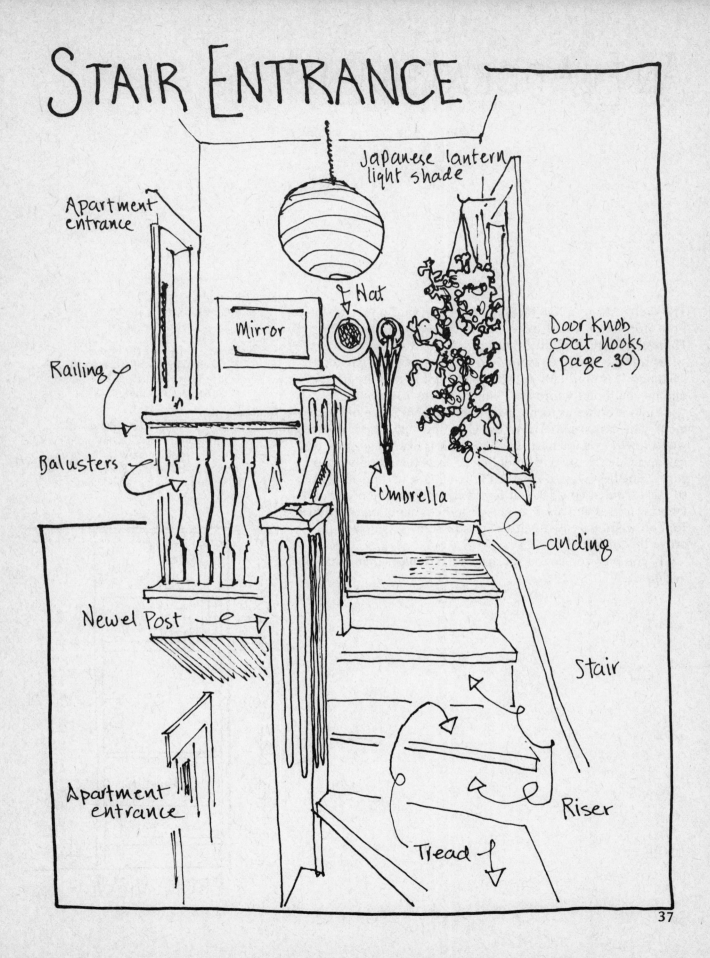

Apartment entrance

Japanese lantern light shade

Hat

Mirror

Door knob coat hooks (page 30)

Railing

Balusters

Umbrella

Landing

Newel Post

Stair

Apartment entrance

Riser

Tread

An Elaborated Entry

The sketch shows a few ideas incorporated into one entry place. For information about the bell, and the window, see p. 26, and 18, respectively. The major part, a seat and cabinet, requires either advanced skill or *meticulous patience* on the part of a beginner. It is especially for the apartment where the front door dumps you directly into the living or dining room.

Build it either as furniture or a permanent piece of the apartment. The easiest material to use is 3/4-inch plywood. Baltic plywood (p. 172) is the best for this, but it is expensive. You can nail and glue flat strips of molding or 1x2s on ugly plywood edges. The best way to cut the plywood is with a portable electric saw, guided by a straight board clamped to the plywood. Use saw horses and another person to help handling the plywood. Join plywood parts with either nails or screws. Glue will improve the joint.

If you plan to use any salvaged parts, collect them before beginning.

Skill Level: Advanced

Tools: Cabinetry

See also: Hanging a Door, p. 176.
Movable Window Shelves, p. 60.
Built-in Greenhouse, p. 62.
Bath Storage Cabinet, p. 104.

Materials:
2 sheets 3/4" x 4' x 8' plywood
Approx. 65 l.f. 1x2 or flat molding
1 lb. 8d finishing nails
Box (50) 1-3/4" no. 8 screws
Titebond or similar wood glue

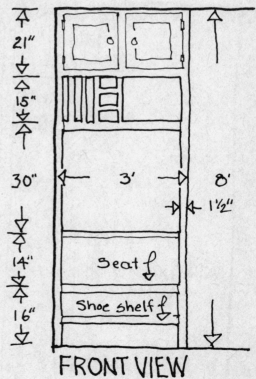

21"
15"
30"
14"
16"
3'
8'
1½"
Seat
Shoe shelf

FRONT VIEW

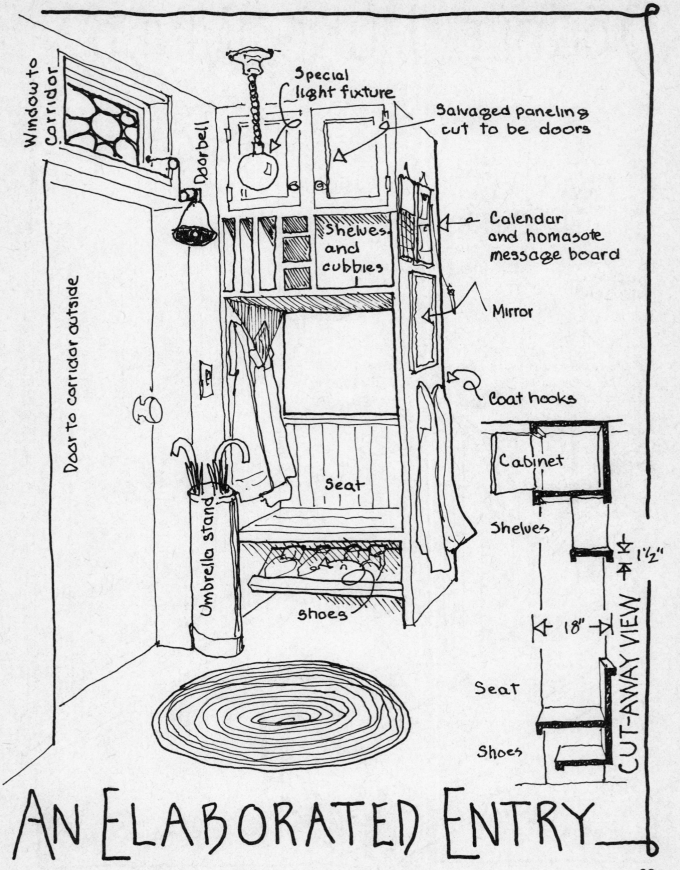

Window to Corridor

Door to corridor outside

Doorbell

Special light fixture

Salvaged paneling cut to be doors

Shelves and cubbies

Calendar and homasote message board

Mirror

Coat hooks

Seat

Umbrella stand

shoes

Cabinet

Shelves

Seat

Shoes

1'½"

18"

CUT-AWAY VIEW

AN ELABORATED ENTRY

Double Hung Window

DETAIL OF LOWER LEFT CORNER

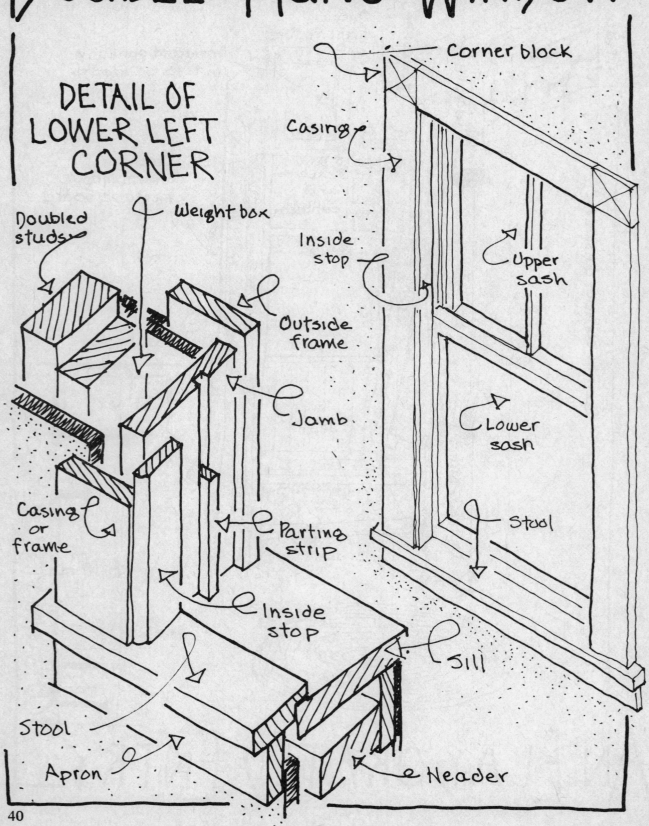

Corner block

Casing

Inside stop

Upper sash

Outside frame

Doubled studs

Weight box

Jamb

Lower sash

Casing or frame

Parting strip

Stool

Inside stop

Sill

Stool

Apron

Header

Windows

The sun travels sparkling in amber glass, moving across floors, walls, changing each day, a calendar. This is another place to build to sit and watch, read, feel the sun, grow gardens of plants and memories. Windows are the eyes of a building.

The pictures here are of an eye mechanism called the double-hung window. Centuries went into its development, and each part has a function — holding sashes in place, balancing their weight (so they won't fall shut when open), keeping out water, covering unsightly edges.

Modern developments of techniques and materials are changing this as the basic window. But it is still the most common window found in homes, so I have mostly used it in this chapter.

STRETCHED FABRIC WINDOW SCREEN

These screens provide all the privacy of curtains or shades, and the added touch of color that may be needed to liven a room. To stretch the fabric, see Stretched Fabric Panels, p. 6. To hang it, screw hooks or eyes into the top of the screen and at the top of the window. The screen can then hook directly to the window or be suspended on wires. In either case, it is simple to remove the screen for access to the window.

Skill Level: Simple

Tools: Hammer
Staple gun (optional)

See also: Stretched Fabric Panels, p. 6.

Materials:
Fabric
4 stretcher strips
Staples or upholstery tacks
2 screw hooks
2 screw eyes

STRETCHED FABRIC WINDOW SCREEN

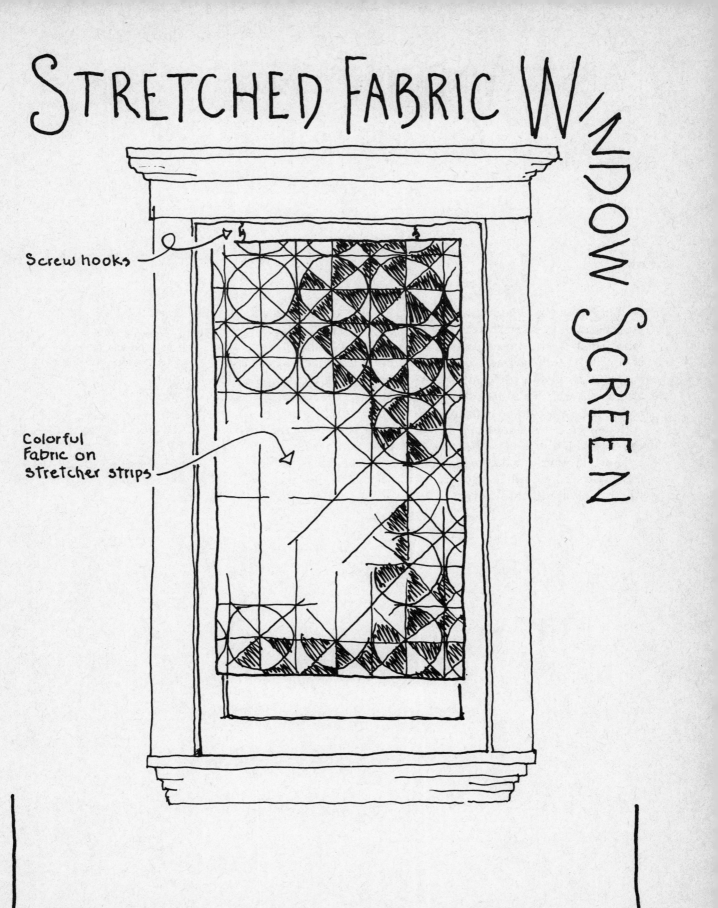

Screw hooks

Colorful Fabric on stretcher strips

FABRIC WINDOW SHADE

If your house has window shades that are worn, but the rollers are still solid, you can replace the old shade with a new. Use fabric. Plain white muslin works very well. You can buy it inexpensively in the garment district (currently less than $1 per yard). Many people use printed fabric with bold patterns. This also works well. To avoid difficulties with the operation of the roller, choose a lightweight fabric. Cut it to width and length, and hem the sides (about one inch). Hem the stick from the bottom of the old shade into the new. A washer with string wrapped around it makes a good pull. Staple the fabric to the roller. Be sure the roller is square with the edge of the fabric or the shade will roll crookedly.

Skill Level: Simple

Tools: Staple gun (expensive to buy, but you can rent one)
Sewing machine, or needle and thread

Materials:
Shade roller and bottom stick
Fabric
String and washer

FABRIC WINDOW SHADE

PRINTED FABRIC

Seam on edge

Window frame

string wrapped around washer

Jan's Colored Window

Jan discovered that while plexiglass colors are poor individually, they are much richer when you combine two layers of different colors. Buy some scraps from a plexiglass dealer, and experiment with colors and patterns. You can cut it by scribing it several times along a straight edge with a razor knife. Then place the piece on a dowel and press down on each side of the scribe mark. A sabre saw with a fine-toothed blade will also cut it. Use the sabre saw to cut curves, too. Sand the edges smooth with a medium sandpaper.

Use a piece of clear plexiglass as a backing to which to attach the smaller pieces. Brush acetone or a plastic cement onto the edges to be joined.

Skill Level: Basic to simple

Tools: Utility or razor knife
Sabre saw (optional, but preferred)

See also: Fabric Window Screen, p. 42.
Window in a Window, p. 48.
Window Through a Wall, p. 18.

Materials:
Plexiglass
Acetone or glue

JAN'S COLORED WINDOW

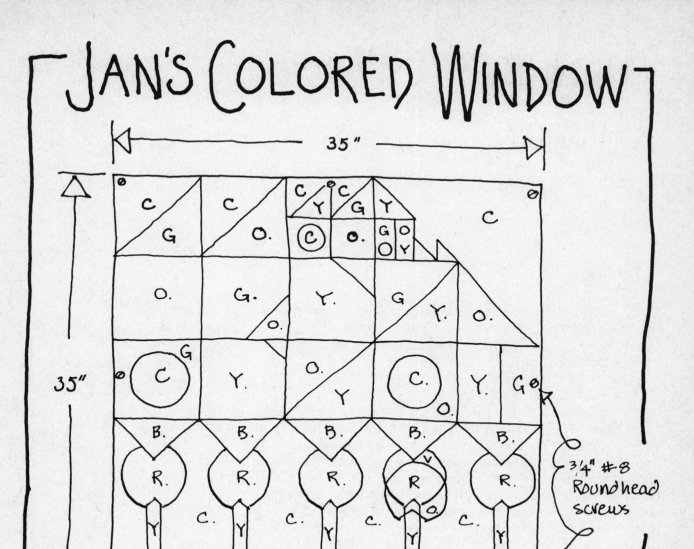

COLORS

Clear Backing - ¼" x 35" x 35" — C.
Green   1/16" thick —   G.
Orange   1/16" thick —   O.
Yellow   1/16" thick —   Y.
Violet   1/16" thick —   V.
Grey   1/16" thick —   B
Red — Violet + Orange —   R

Colored window made to be same size as existing Sash. & fastened to it with round-head wood screws

¾" #8 Round head screws

Window in a Window

If you are fortunate enough to find some stained or leaded glass and have the energy to save it, or the money to buy, this is something to do with it. The window mounted inside a window frame is another substitute for curtains. The sketch shows two ways to mount the found window.

The most elegant method requires two threaded rods, four nuts and washers, and four metal clamps to clamp the two rods to the frame. The threaded rod should be about 1-1/2 inches greater in length than the distance between the two window stops. (The window stops are those 1/2 by 2 or 3-inch strips that are screwed to the inside sides and top of the window frame.) Attach the rods across the stained glass with clamps and screws (see the drawing). Measure the distance between the rods and drill four holes into the window frame. Spin the nuts and washers well onto the rod. If the holes are sufficiently deep it will be possible to insert one end of the rods and then to slide the assembly back the other way. Tighten the nuts to prevent movement.

The other method is less elegant and more obvious. Screw two 1x2s to the back of the stained glass. Then attach these to the window stops with angle irons. It's probably a good idea to fit the 1x2s to the angles to set the screws, then to remove the angles, screw them to the stops, set the window assembly on the angles, and rescrew them into place.

Skill Level: Basic

Tools: Drill, screwdriver, measure

Materials:
  2 3/8" threaded metal rods
  4 metal clamps
  4 3/8" hex nuts and washers
  8 screws

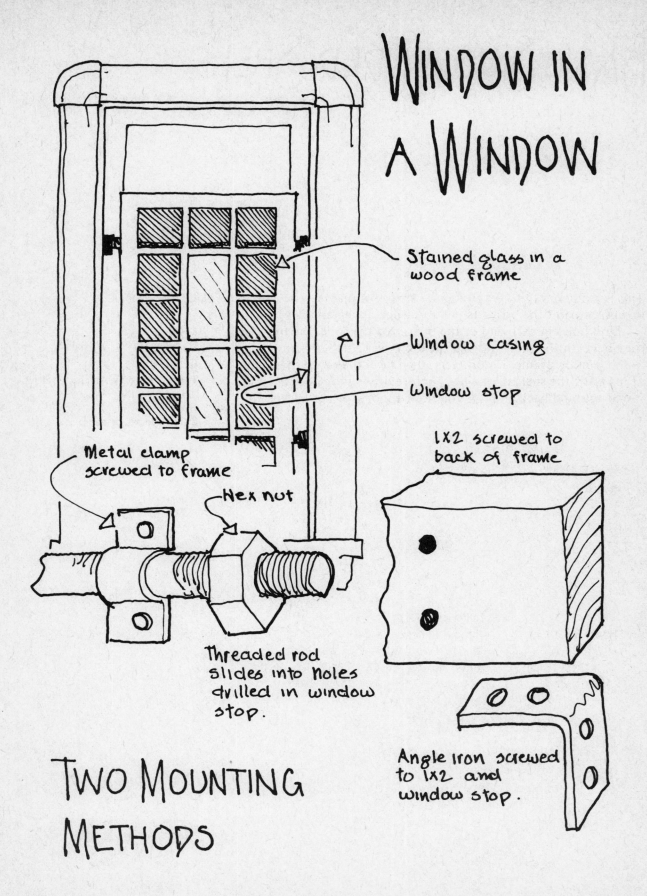

WINDOW IN A WINDOW

Stained glass in a wood frame

Window casing

Window stop

Metal clamp screwed to frame

Hex nut

1X2 screwed to back of frame

Threaded rod slides into holes drilled in window stop.

Angle iron screwed to 1x2 and window stop.

TWO MOUNTING METHODS

Basic Suspended Shelf

This is a quick way to get storage or space for plants. You can varnish or paint the board to get a finished appearance.

Drill holes in each end of the board for the rope. Tie the rope beneath the shelf and slip the loop over a nail or screwhook in the window frame. Do one end, then level the other by raising or lowering the shelf till it's level before driving the hook. Get a friend to stand back and tell you how it looks, or use a level.

Skill Level: Simple

Tools: Drill
Level
Hammer (if you use nails)

Materials:
1 board longer than the window
frame is wide
Rope
2 screwhooks or nails

BASIC SUSPENDED SHELF

Screwhook
in window
frame

Hooks on bottom
of shelf

Screwhook

1x8 Board

SHELF SUSPENDED
IN WINDOW FRAME

Rope knotted on bottom of shelf

Line of window frame

51

LIGHT AND SHADOW

The sun moves in an ever-changing yet constant arc. The ancients discovered the rhythm, and built monument calendars like Stonehenge. They invented the sundial also. The sun's arc changes each day, yet a sundial tells the correct time.

My third-floor bedroom has windows facing east. Since I have lived here for a few years, I have noticed how the sun changes with seasons. Last spring was marvelous, for I was anticipating the sun's movements. I put things in my windows — many plants as well as articles that reflect light. The light bounces and shimmers, casting shadows through a leafy veil, shadows that shimmer and move with the sun and the morning breeze. At 7:30 a programmed reflection slips onto my bed. The cat crawls into it to sleep. I rouse from slumber to see.

See also:
Fabric Window Shade, p. 44.
Shelf in Window, p. 56.
Sundial, p. 58.

LIGHT AND SHADOW

Light from mirror plays on radiating lines painted on ceiling representing half hour intervals.

Circular mirrors hung on strings

Sundial mirror

Colored glass

Fresnel lens

Bottles

Fabric window shade

Shelves

Cat in sunlight

Bed posts made from old newell posts found in abandoned houses

Rod and Brackets

Plants will grow to be roommates and curtains. An arrangement of plants hung from a rod is more flexible than one hung from individual brackets. It is important to keep the plants far enough away from the window — eight inches from the pot center to the window has been sufficient for me. Less than that is too crowded; the plants get burned by the sun and touched by the cold, and the window shade is hard to operate. Cut the bracket out of wood. Decide on a shape, cut curves with a sabre saw, then then file and sand. The rod is a closet pole about 1-1/4 inches in diameter, but a broomstick will work also. The hole for the rod is drilled with an appropriate speed bore bit in an electric drill. If the window frame is the wood type, 1-1/2- to 2-inch no. 8 screws will hold the bracket in place. If the house is old, it is possible that the window is no longer level. Don't assume that by measuring equal distances down from the top of the window the rod will be level. Get someone to help you set the bracket heights by eye.

Skill Level: Basic to simple.

Tools: Basic tools
   Sabre saw (optional)

See also: Molly Bolts and Expansion
      Shields, p. 174.
   Shelf in Window, p. 56.

Materials:
   2 l.f. 1x6 or plywood
   4 1-1/2 or 2" no. 8 screws
   4 ft. closet pole or broomstick

ROD AND BRACKETS

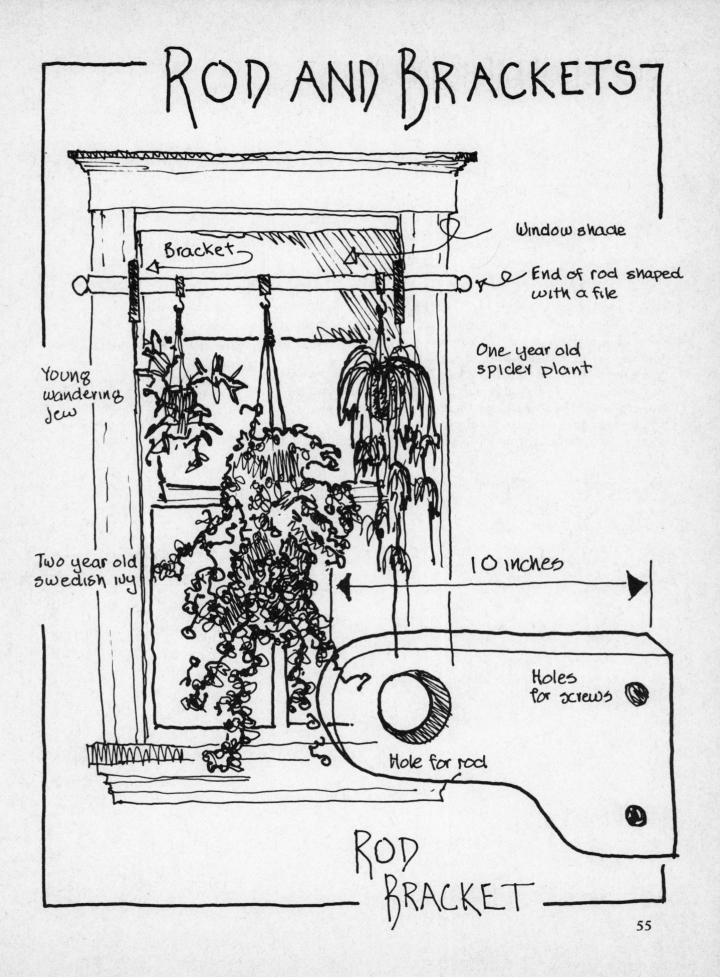

Window shade

End of rod shaped with a file

Bracket

One year old spider plant

Young wandering Jew

Two year old swedish ivy

10 inches

Holes for screws

Hole for rod

ROD BRACKET

SHELF IN WINDOW

This is an addition to the rod and bracket idea. The bracket needs to be designed to carry a shelf as well as a rod. Attach the bracket to the window frame in the same way, using screws. The shelf doesn't have to be a single board but can be strips, and it isn't necessary to attach it to the brackets. The location of the brackets is important. The window should still be operable and the brackets should be low enough to allow access to the plants, but high enough not to interfere. In this case, they are high enough to permit a view out the window while seated in a chair next to it.

Skill Level: Basic

Tools: Basic

See also: Rod and Brackets, p. 54.

Materials:
 2 l.f. 1x10 or plywood board or wood strips for shelf
 closet pole or broom stick
 4 1-1/2" or 2" no. 8 screws

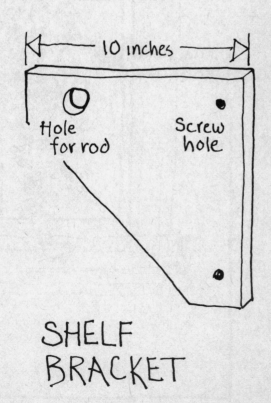

10 inches

Hole for rod

Screw hole

SHELF BRACKET

SHELF IN WINDOW

Herbs in a planter box

Shelf

Rod

Shelf bracket

SUNDIAL

The sun's reflection into a room from off a mirror (piece of glass, metal, someone else's window, china) traces a daily changing path. The path has extremes around June 22 and December 22 (the solstices). In winter the sun is low and will reach deep into the room; in summer, the opposite will happen. The reflected paths move west to east. You can calibrate the motion by marking lines or a pattern that corresponds to hourly changes. Complete accuracy would be tedious, but the idea of inviting the sun to take part in home decoration is not difficult to implement. Locate a mirror(s) or objects that reflect sunlight into the room, leaving them in the same position for the half year between solstices, and notice what the sun's reflection does. Take a sunny morning (afternoon) near the solstices and equinox to mark pertinent hourly positions of the sun on the wall or ceiling. The pattern will easily relate to the sun design but will be shifted from the room's center. The flames could be in different lengths and colors — red, orange, yellow — corresponding to winter, fall, and spring, and summer sun arcs. Or the design could be more abstract — perhaps bands of color reaching up the wall and across the ceiling, tracing the paths of the sun during holidays or birthdays.

See also: Light and Shadow, p. 52.

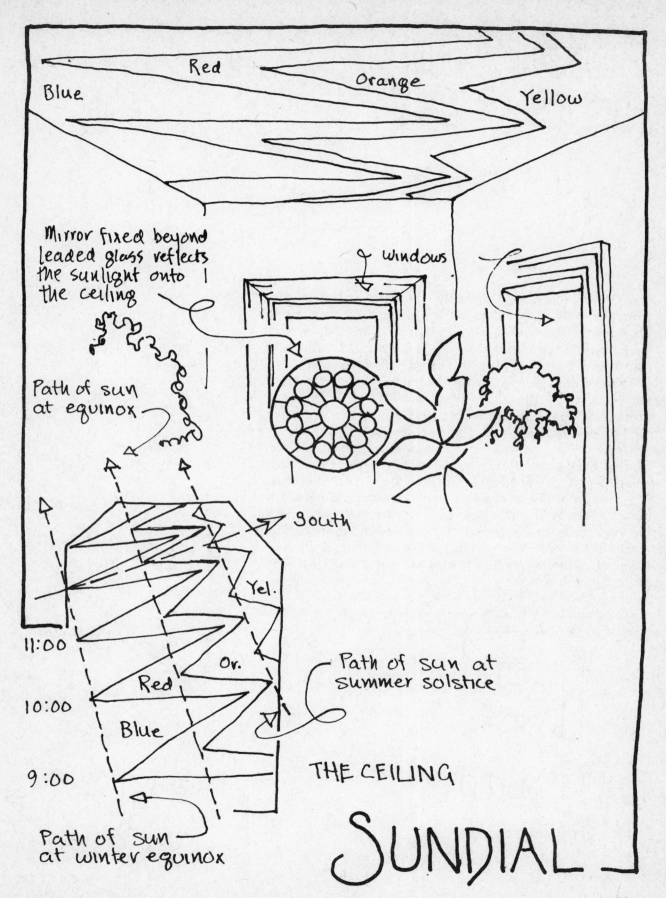

Blue   Red   Orange   Yellow

Mirror fixed beyond
leaded glass reflects
the sunlight onto
the ceiling

windows

Path of sun
at equinox

South

Yel.

11:00

Or.

Path of sun at
summer solstice

Red

10:00

Blue

9:00

THE CEILING

Path of sun
at winter equinox

SUNDIAL

MOVABLE WINDOW SHELVES

This drawing shows a shelving system built into a type of window commonly found in modern apartments and dormitories. The window frame is deep enough to house wide shelves which can be used for decoration, storage, and privacy. A shade is hung below waist level for added privacy when necessary.

To build this system, first cut the frame boards (two sides and possibly a top for the sake of appearance). Place the boards edge-to-edge and mark them simultaneously for the drilling of shelf-support holes. The shelf support shown is sold at many hardware stores, and while it functions in the same fashion as clip-and-track supports, it is considerably cheaper. Be sure that holes are perfectly lined up or shelves will not be flat. Permanently screw or bolt boards to the window frame. Shelves can be positioned at desirable heights. The lower shelves in front of the shade are narrower to permit the raising and lowering of the shade. If shelves are to span much more than thirty inches, either add a central support or use thicker material, such as 2" stock, for shelves.

Skill Level: Basic

Tools: Basic Kit

Materials:
- 2 1x12s, 3/4" less than height of window
- 1 1x12, as wide as window
- 2 1x12s, 1-3/4" less than width of window
- 2 1x8s, 1-3/4" less than width of window
- 16 shelf supports
- 12 Molly bolts

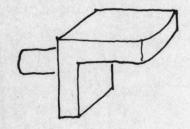

SHELF SUPPORT

(Bigger than actual size)

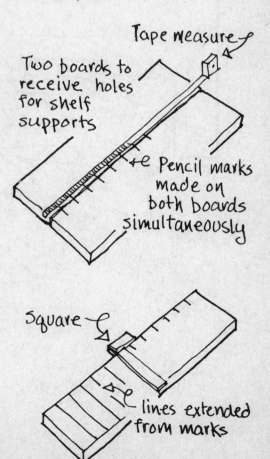

Tape measure

Two boards to receive holes for shelf supports

Pencil marks made on both boards simultaneously

Square

lines extended from marks

MOVABLE WINDOW SHELVES

Wind chimes

Terrarium

Shade hung below shelf

Shells

Toys

Wood frame permanently bolted to window frame

Shelf support

Holes drilled at regular intervals for shelf supports

DETAIL OF SHELVES

Pine 1x12's

SHELF SUPPORT

(Bigger than actual size)

Built-In Greenhouse

Basically, this is a box built to fit inside the window frame. To install the box, remove the inside stops and slide the box into their place. Screwed to the sides of the window frame, the box will serve the function of stops, and will be removable for repairs to the window.

First, find glass doors or windows which are at least 1½ inches narrower than the full width of the sash. (If the sash is 34 inches wide, then the width of the two doors together should be less than 32-1/2 inches.) Build a box that will slide into the window frame, allowing a 1/8-inch margin for error. The drawing shows a box with an upper compartment separated from a lower compartment by a fixed shelf. The lower compartment is tall enough to have an adjustable shelf in it. Follow the method described in "Movable Window Shelves" (p. 60). Join the top, bottom, sides, and fixed shelf with nails or screws.

As drawn, the box is sufficiently larger than the doors to permit strips of wood to trim the front edges of the box. These "stiles" are nailed and glued to the box. The stiles that are to hold hinges could be fitted with the hinges first. This seems to make that step easier. To attach hinges, see p. 174.

Skill Level: Basic to advanced

Tools: Cabinetry

See also: Hanging a Door, p. 176.
Bath Storage Cabinet, p. 104.
Built-in Storage, p. 16.

Materials: (for 36" x 60" greenhouse)
2 1" x 12" x 36"
2 1" x 12" x 58-1/2"
1 1" x 12" x 34-1/2"
1 1" x 12" x 34-1/2"
3 1" x 2" x 36"
2 1" x 2" x 15"
2 1" x 2" x 41-1/2"
3 doors
6 hinges
6 1-1/2" or 2" no. 8 screws
1 lb. 8d finishing nails
Wood glue

BUILT-IN GREENHOUSE

Existing window frame

Colored glass window hinged at top

Fixed shelf dividing two compartments inside

Adjustable shelf inside see "Movable Windowshelves"

Screw hole for attaching box to window frame

Pine 1×12's or 3/4" plywood for sides, top shelves, & bottom.

Pair of dining room cabinet doors from salvage yard

CONSTRUCTION DETAIL

Window Seat

This drawing may look complex, but the project is actually quite easy. The sketch shows a seat built along the narrow end of a glassed-in porch and finished in the same manner as the walls and trim of the porch. It can be constructed from used lumber. Sixteen inches with the cushion is a comfortable height. The width will vary depending upon use — if it is to be a guest bed, for example, you might make it about two feet wide.

Build the base first. Nail short 2x3s between two long 2x3s as a bottom for the storage compartment. Next, build the front and back: two more 2x3s supported by the same. The front and back are tied together with 2x3s and braced with a diagonal. A 1x3 trims the top edge on all four sides. The exposed front can either be wood or plasterboard. The seat bottoms are 3/4-inch plywood.

Skill Level: Basic

Tools: Basic

Materials: (for 6'x2' seat)
  48 l.f. 1x3
  2 pieces 2'x6' plywood
  16 l.f. 1x3
  5 s.f. wainscot
  1/2 lb. 8d common nails
  1/2 lb. 10d common nails
  1/2 lb. 8d finishing nails
  1/4 lb. 6d common nails

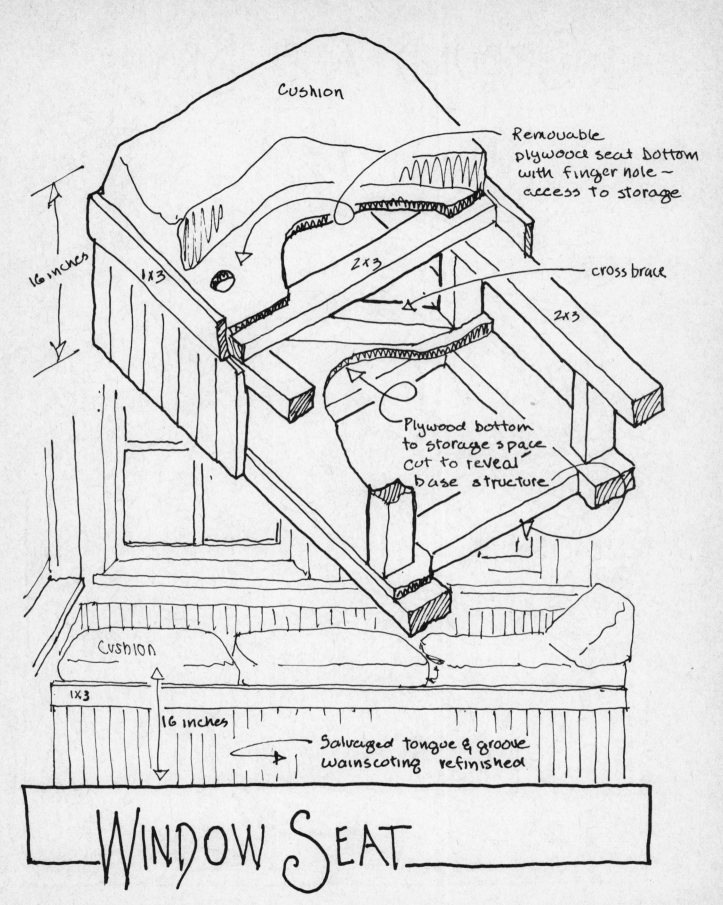

Cushion

Removable
plywood seat bottom
with finger hole —
access to storage

16 inches

1x3

2x3

cross brace

2x3

Plywood bottom
to storage space
cut to reveal
base structure

Cushion

1x3

16 inches

Salvaged tongue & groove
wainscoting refinished

WINDOW SEAT

GROUND AND SKY

GROUND AND SKY

This is the first of the chapters that also applies to collaborative projects done by groups of building residents. Old cities have more bricks and mosaics than newer cities. These fine materials were once economically feasible. Somehow we can't afford them now. But we could do it ourselves. The concrete and asphalt around our buildings are good foundations for more imaginative surfaces. The same is true inside. Time, skill, availability of materials, and resources may limit the size of projects. But even a little garden is better than no garden.

Frustrated at efforts to be constructively creative, many people become destructively creative. Some people revolt and remain creative in spite of pressures against them: a bricklayer makes brickwork patterns where randomness was mandated; children render chalk-colored drawings on asphalt; "hoodlum" artists decorate subway cars.

PAVING

This project is for outside. At an apartment building it would probably be done collectively. As drawn, it shows an entry with a grid of bricks forming a square into which broken bricks and stones are placed. Plan the grid so that it works for the brick sizes. Lay it out carefully with all corners square if possible. Use stakes and string to mark the grid.

The best base is concrete. Asphalt or ground will also work, but these will tend to heave over the years. Place a two-inch depth of sand on the base. Position the grid, then fill in the squares. Individuals could do separate squares. Once everything is placed, wet it down gently to moisten and settle the bricks and sand. Use a broom to brush the 3:1 sand-cement mixture into the joints. Hose the surface gently again, wait 15 minutes, and repeat.

Skill Level: Basic

Tools: Shovel
  Rake
  Hammer
  Masonry chisel
  Hose with nozzle

Materials:
  Bricks
  Stones
  Sand
  Portland cement

PAVING

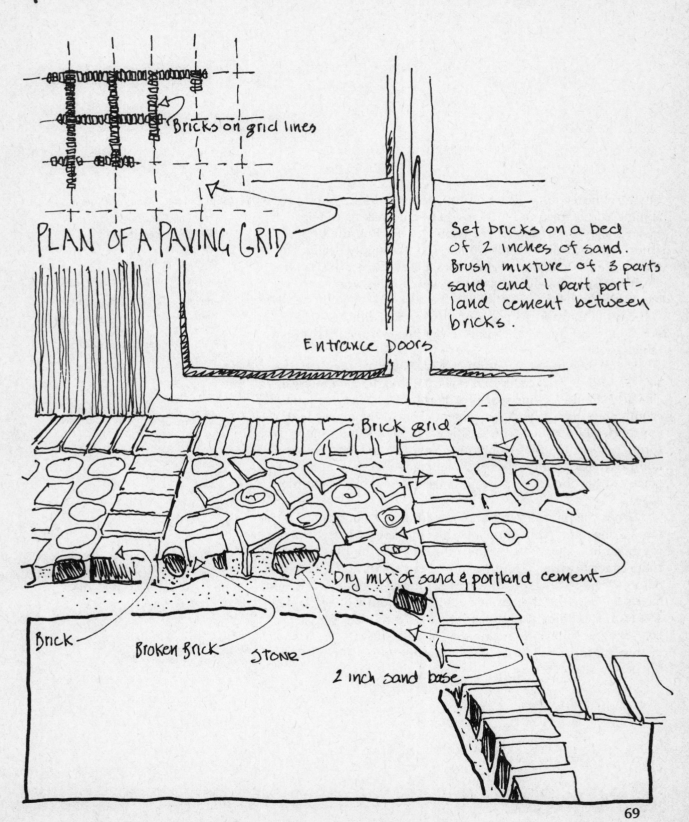

Bricks on grid lines

PLAN OF A PAVING GRID

Set bricks on a bed of 2 inches of sand. Brush mixture of 3 parts sand and 1 part portland cement between bricks.

Entrance Doors

Brick grid

Brick

Broken Brick

Stone

Dry mix of sand & portland cement

2 inch sand base

Quarry Tile Floor

These are heavy-duty ceramic tiles. Modern mastics (glues) have eliminated the need to set them in cement, making the process easy enough for inexperienced people to do. Buy the tiles, grout, and specialized tools from a flooring supply dealer. Do shop around for a good deal on tiles, because the price can be absurd. Also, talk with contractors who do this work — they may have some leftovers they'd sell cheap. Try to find one who will cut the tiles for the edges of the room. (Failing this, it is possible to cut quarry tiles yourself with a masonry blade on a table saw.)

Follow the preparations on p. 177. Since the tiles vary in size, I prefer to strike a grid of lines at about 12-inch intervals. The grid should include space for 1/4- to 3/8-inch-wide joints for grout, a mixture of sand and cement. Spread the mastic with the appropriately notched trowel. The chalk lines should show through. Place the tiles firmly in the mastic, and work so you don't have to stand on tiles you've already placed. Kneel on a piece of plywood to measure and mark tiles to be cut for the edges.

Grout the joints after 24 hours with gray floor grout. To obtain lasting joints, follow the mixing directions exactly. Force the grout into the joints by smearing it across the tiles with a rubber faced trowel. Grout no more than about 100 square feet before cleaning the faces of the tiles. However, be sure the joints have set enough so that grout doesn't come out while you clean. The joint should be flush. Clean the tiles with water and a coarse rag or sponge, changing the water frequently. A second or third cleaning will be necessary to remove the film left by the grout.

Skill Level: Basic (but messy work)

Tools: Notched trowel
Rubber-faced trowel
Coarse rags
Plastic bucket

See also: General Preparations, p. 177.

Materials: (after preparation)
Quarry tiles
Mastic
Paint thinner for cleanup
Gray floor grout

QUARRY TILE FLOOR

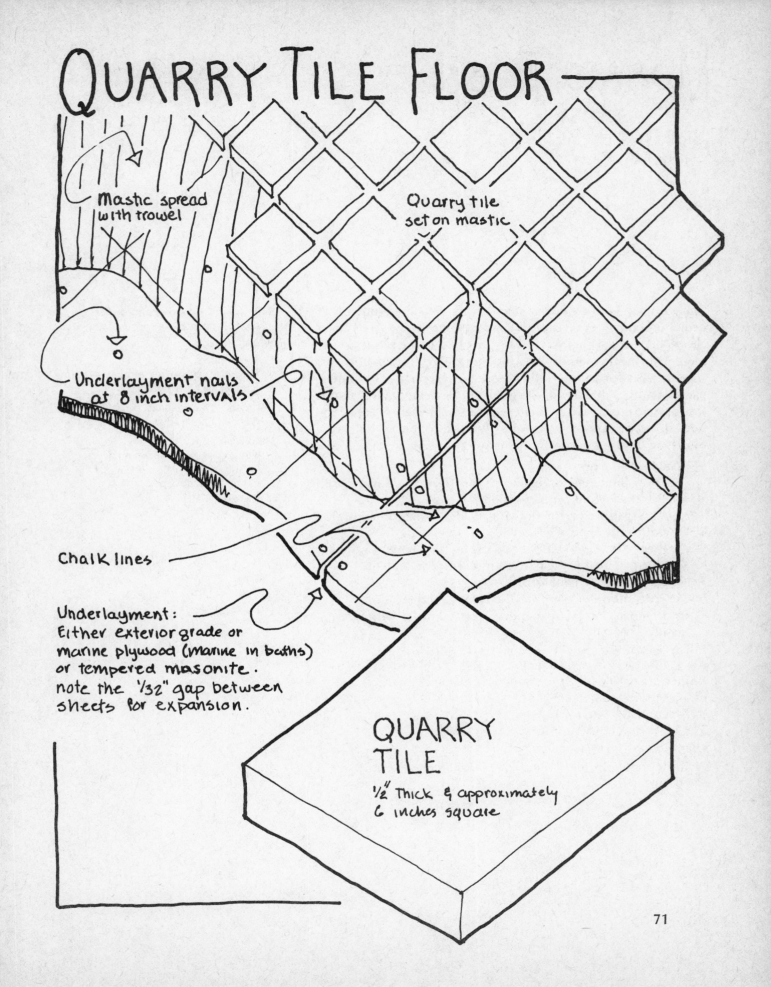

Mastic spread with trowel

Quarry tile set on mastic

Underlayment nails at 8 inch intervals

Chalk lines

Underlayment:
Either exterior grade or marine plywood (marine in baths) or tempered masonite.
note the 1/32" gap between sheets for expansion.

QUARRY TILE
1/2" Thick & approximately 6 inches square

Mosaic Tiles

This idea was used by Pedro Silva (an artist) and a group of neighborhood volunteers at the park around Grant's Tomb in New York City. The process was described to me by a participant. The mastic method described for quarry tiles *might* work with mosaics for an interior surface. However, that technique placed the tiles directly in tile grout or tile cement, and an outside mosaic must have a concrete base. A sidewalk is great. Inside, a base of exterior or marine plywood topped with a layer of plastic (a vapor barrier) is advised.

The procedure:
1. Draw the design on brown paper. (Discover a manageable size through experimentation.)
2. Arrange tiles on the drawing. "Tiles" might include glass, pot chards, and shells.
3. Press clear Con-tact paper onto the tiles so you will be able to transfer the pattern intact to the cement.
4. Spread tile cement with a trowel.
5. Press sheets of tiles into the cement and let it dry.
6. Remove Con-tact paper and grout joints as with quarry tile.

Skill Level: An experienced tiler to coordinate the work is recommended.

Tools: Scissors
Tile nippers
Trowels for trowling cement
Rubber-faced trowel

See Also: Quarry Tiles, p. 70.
General Preparation, p. 177.

Materials:
Tiles, glass, pot chards, shells
Grout
Clear Con-tact paper
Brown paper

Design for mosaic drawn
on brown paper and cut
into manageable sizes.
Tiles arranged onto
brown paper drawing.
Design lifted from
brown paper with
clear contact paper.

LAYING-OUT MOSAIC

Tiles on clear contact
paper pushed into
cement.
Peel contact paper off
when cement has dried.

Tile cement

Concrete, or exterior
grade plywood with a
vapor barrier on top.

PLACING TILES
IN CEMENT

MOSAIC TILES

Jan's Puzzle Floor

This is a difficult project. It may be most appropriate either in your own home, or in a public area of a large apartment building. Due to the project's complexity, the area should be small — an entry area, hall, stair landing, small room, elevator, or lobby, for instance. Jan's floor is a collection of different kinds of wood with some old factory-made block alphabet letters, printing blocks, wooden medallions, and a collection of 50 two-inch squares carved by his friends. (*See* p. 166)

Steps:

1. Prepare the floor. Cover a standard wood floor with exterior plywood securely nailed in place with underlayment nails. A concrete floor should be bump free.

2. Map the puzzle onto the floor determining the number of pieces, sizes of major pieces, and locations for special ones. Use a chalk line to lay out a grid of lines to help keep parts properly aligned during the laying process.

3. Cut the pieces on a table saw. Their sizes must be accurate to within a few thousandths of an inch.

4. Spread contact cement on the floor for about a 10-square-foot area, and on the backs of all but the special pieces.

5. Wait 10 or 15 minutes and set the cement covered pieces.

6. Repeat the last two steps until you have covered the rest of the floor.

7. Fit special pieces and label them so you will know where to to glue them later.

8. Sand the floor even with a commercial floor sander.

9. Glue the special pieces in place.

10. Apply at least three coats of polyurethane finish or oil floor sealer following instructions on the can.

Skill Level: Complex

Tools: Basic tools, plus
Table saw
Mallet or soft-faced hammer
Brush (to spread contact cement)
Belt sander to make minor size adjusments in special pieces
Rent commercial floor sander

Also see: General Preparation, p. 177.

Materials:
Oak
Maple
Mahogany
Cherry
Teak
Special pieces
Contact cement
Polyurethane or oil sealer for floors

JAN'S PUZZLE FLOOR

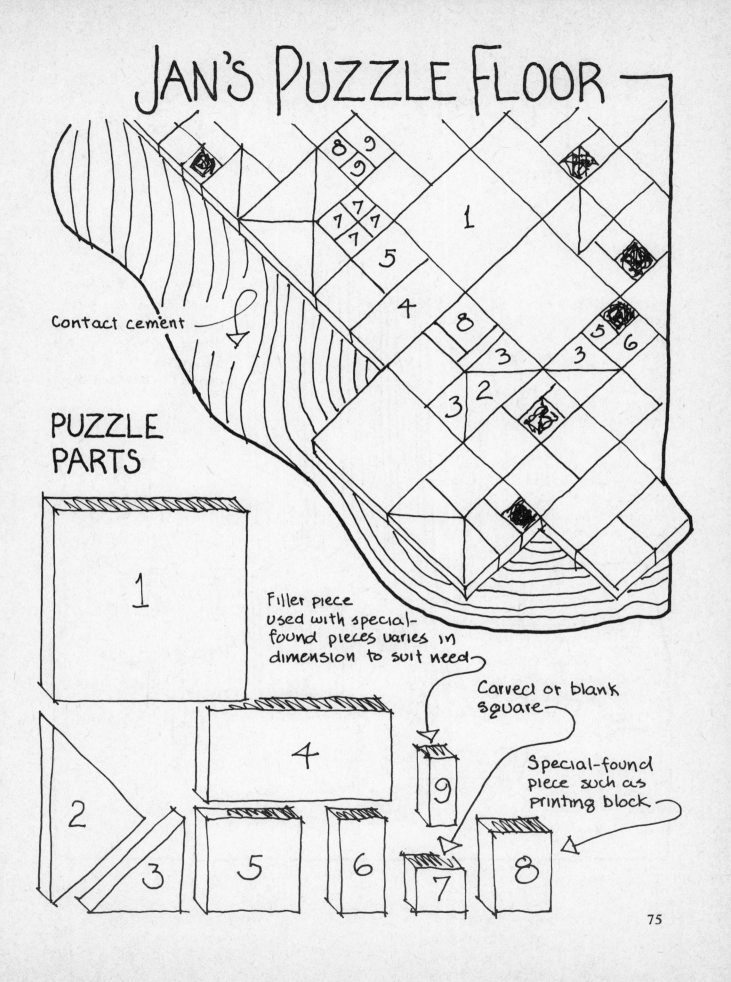

Contact cement

PUZZLE
PARTS

1

2

3

4

5

6

7

8

9

Filler piece used with special-found pieces varies in dimension to suit need

Carved or blank square

Special-found piece such as printing block

PUBLIC PLACES

A group of neighbors constructing a place to sit & hang plants in the laundry of their apartment building

PUBLIC PLACES

Like the ground and sky of our new buildings, the public spaces
are often blank. The projects that follow are larger and more
advanced than projects found elsewhere in this book. They
apply to buildings where there are empty public spaces, and are
likely to be collaborative efforts. They can be accomplished
through a pooling of skills, efforts, resources, some money, and
the direction of one or more people who take charge (at least
on a technical level) to ensure that *ideas* become *realities*. The
person in charge will be a kind of architect. (S)he will need many
of the skills an architect uses. This "family architect" will need
to know about putting things together, understanding other
people's ideas, organizing a work force, and when and where
to consult professional builders. An old carpenter or contractor,
a hardware-store owner, a handy person, an architecture student — these are possible family architects. By working together
you can learn about each other, as well as about building.

Entrance Trellis

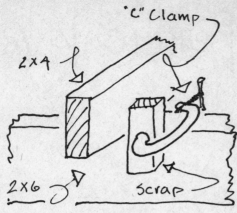

METHOD FOR KEEPING 2X4 IN POSITION WHILE BEING TOENAILED

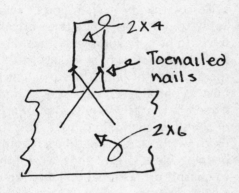

This is a simpler trellis than many to make. The drawing shows an easy way to set posts. It would be easier but less secure to set the posts without the concrete collar. It would also be possible to make concrete footings and to anchor the posts to them. But setting the posts in the ground eliminates the need for cross bracing.

You can buy the concrete in ready-to-add-water mixtures. Carefully set posts so they are perfectly vertical, and they line up with each other. Trim them so their tops are level after they are in the ground. (This way you can forget about the sloping ground and holes of slightly differing depths.)

The 2x6 beams bolt into notches in the tops of the 4x4 posts. Use 3/8" x 4-inch carriage bolts. "Toenail" the 2x4s to the 2x6s with 8d galvanized nails.

For lumber, redwood is best. Treat it with a wood preservative such as Cuprinol, especially the posts that will go into the ground. You can also use salvaged lumber. Used yellow pine is good and costs about one-third as much as redwood.

Skill Level: Basic

Tools: Basic and digging tools.

See also: Fence, p. 80.

Materials:
  4 4" x 4" x 10' posts
  2 2" x 6" x 8' beams
  7 2" x 4" x 8" joists
  8 3/8" x 4" carriage bolts with nuts
     and washers
  1/2 lb. 8d common galvanized nails
  Wood preservative
  Readymix concrete
  Gravel

ENTRANCE TRELLIS

2×6

4×4
Post

PERSPECTIVE
SKETCH

Entrance
Door

2×4's

Carriage
Bolts

2×6

CONSTRUCTION
DETAIL

4×4
Post

Concrete
collar

Fence ties into post

3 foot
(min.)

Gravel surrounds lower portion
of post

79

FENCE

Redwood, cedar, and yellow pine are rot resistant in that order, and are proper materials for fence posts. The availability and price will depend on where you live. When treated with Cuprinol, a 4x4 post may last in the ground 30 years or more. The hardest part of putting up a fence is getting the posts in line. Use string stretched between the corner locations to do this. A line level will help ascertain the amount of slope in the ground. The vertical strips in this drawing are yellow pine flooring. Either sand the old finish off or let the weather do it for you after the fence is up. You can paint it later.

Note: Use galvanized nails for all exterior work.

Skill Level: Basic

Tools: Basic, line level, and digging tools

See also: Trellis, p. 78.

Materials:
- 4x4 posts
- 2x4 crosspieces
- 1x4s or old flooring
- Wood preservative
- 10d galvanized common nails for crosspieces
- 6d galvanized common nails for 1x4s
- Readymix concrete
- Gravel

FENCE

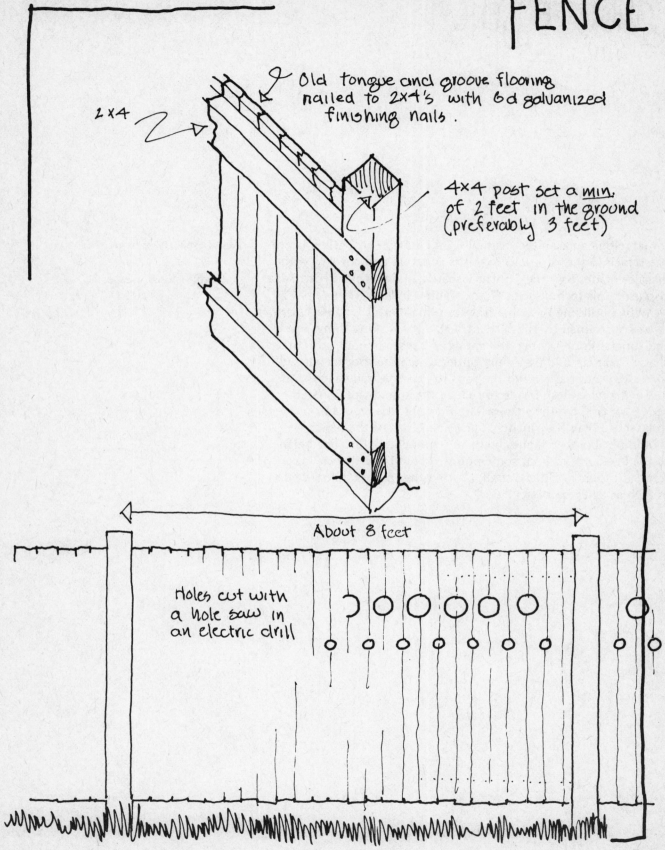

Old tongue and groove flooring nailed to 2×4's with 6d galvanized finishing nails.

2×4

4×4 post set a <u>min.</u> of 2 feet in the ground (preferably 3 feet)

About 8 feet

Holes cut with a hole saw in an electric drill

CONCRETE BENCH

In Barcelona an architect named Gaudi built a serpentine, lizard-like bench in the Parque Guell. It is concrete and covered with mosaics made from tiles, pottery shards, and marble. Pedro Silva also used this technique at Grant's Tomb in New York City.

When building in such a free-form manner, it isn't necessary to be constrained by the carpentry rules of making things level and square. Pour a concrete footing and insert metal rods purchased from a building-supply outlet. Once the footing has set for a couple of days, bend the rods to their desired shapes and suspend a wire mesh inside to reduce the amount of concrete necessary to form the shapes. The final thickness doesn't need to be more than four inches. The dimensions of the bench should be about 16 inches high, and 16 inches wide. The height of the back can vary: at some points it could be at elbow-rest level, at others not there at all; at still other points it could be as high as a person's back.

Skill Level: Prior experience with concrete

See also: Mosaic tiles, p. 72.

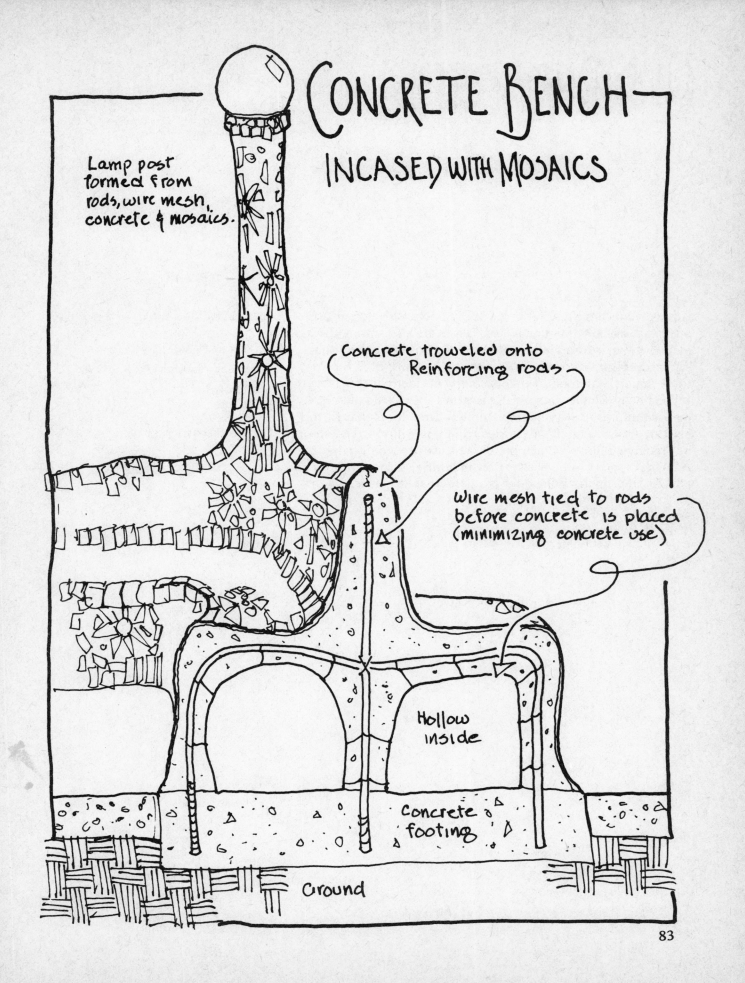

Concrete Bench
Incased with Mosaics

Lamp post formed from rods, wire mesh, concrete & mosaics.

Concrete troweled onto Reinforcing rods

Wire mesh tied to rods before concrete is placed (minimizing concrete use)

Hollow inside

Concrete footing

Ground

Old Doors

Salvage yards are a good source for old doors, since doors are highly salvageable building pieces. Doors are also among the most individual parts of buildings. Newer buildings have plain doors. Apartments and dormitories are especially guilty of harboring these impersonal doors. Tenants could consider collaborating to get some "new" old doors if the existing ones have fallen into poor condition. It may be impossible to find doors that fit the existing frames exactly. Excessive trimming will weaken a door, but removing up to an inch on all sides usually won't harm it. Hanging a door can be tricky. Consider hiring a carpenter for the job. An improperly hung door is a perpetual headache.

Skill Level: Advanced

Tools: Cabinetry Kit
Portable power saw

See also: Hanging a Door, p. 176.

Materials:
Doors
Hinges
Doorknobs, locks, etc.

An existing entrance in modern steel with the addition of an old salvaged wooden door and stained glass.

TELEPHONE INTERCOM PANEL

A common telephone intercom panel we've all seen is a plain piece of plywood fastened into an existing window frame between the lobby and vestibule. It's ugly from the inside and impersonal from the outside. It wouldn't cost much more to use a piece of Baltic plywood instead. This looks better right away. You could cut a design through the plywood, like the one shown. I have seen designs cut through Baltic plywood with great success. To keep it from breaking, consider using some extra stiffener such as the frame drawn here. If you design the pattern (or copy the one shown) expecting to attach it to a frame, you'll be okay. Draw the design, drill holes for the sabre saw blade. Use a fine-toothed blade, cut slowly, backing up whenever necessary, and smooth the cuts with sandpaper and files. This is also a good window screen option to curtains for privacy.

Skill Level: Basic

Tools: Basic and sabre saw

Materials:
- 1/2" x 2" x 30" Baltic plywood
- 2 1" x 2" x 8' pine, birch, or oak for frame
- 20 1-1/4" no. 8 screws to attach plywood to frame
- 1/4 lb. 6d finishing nails for connecting frame parts.

TELEPHONE INTERCOM PANEL

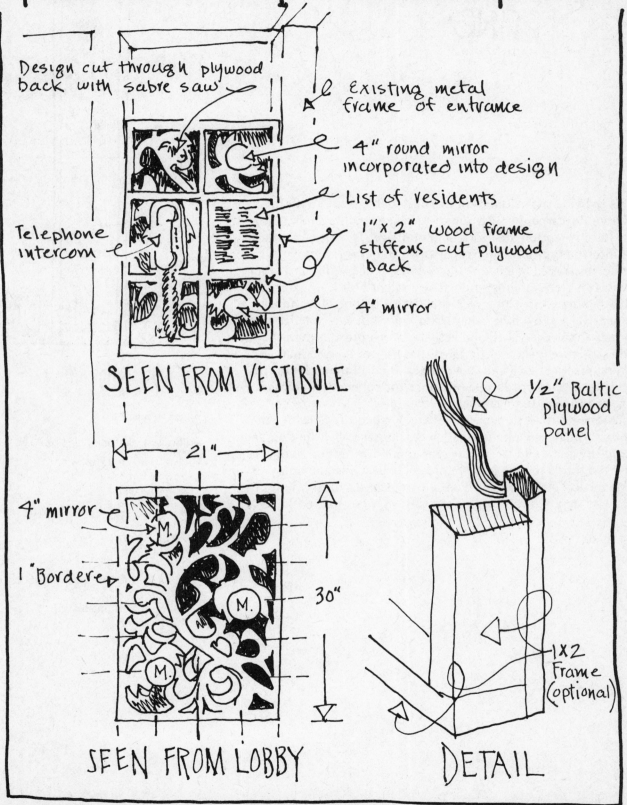

Design cut through plywood back with sabre saw

Telephone intercom

SEEN FROM VESTIBULE

Existing metal frame of entrance

4" round mirror incorporated into design

List of residents

1" x 2" wood frame stiffens cut plywood back

4" mirror

½" Baltic plywood panel

4" mirror

1" Border

21"

30"

SEEN FROM LOBBY

1 X 2 Frame (optional)

DETAIL

Place for Plants
& Sitting

This drawing shows one way to build such a place. With the help of a young carpenter, a group of teenagers built a similar structure as a reception area for a school office. The idea might also fit into the typical modern apartment building lobby with hard floor, suspended acoustical tile ceilings, block walls, and much glass. It is free-standing, though you might bolt it down to protect climbers. Fir with a varnished finish is gorgeous, though expensive. Yellow pine is harder to work but available for less money in salvage yards, and actually much prettier than the fir. The structure is six 2x4 uprights that bolt to longitudinal and lateral pieces of 2x6 and 2x4 lumber. Predrill the holes in the uprights at the appropriate locations for connection points. Clamp the longitudinal pieces to the uprights, checking for squareness with a carpenter's square. Extend the holes for the bolts through the longitudinal pieces. Dissasemble the clamped structure and build the ladder, the frame for the seat supports, and the frame for the bottom piece. Reassemble and apply 1x4 vertical strips and horizontal trim. Cut decorative holes as a last step before applying the varnish. (*See* p. 164.)

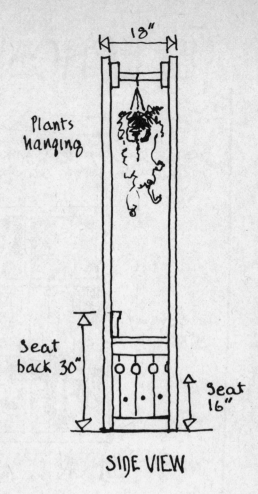

18"

Plants hanging

Seat back 30"

Seat 16"

SIDE VIEW

Skill Level: Difficult side of Basic

Tools: Basic and ripsaw
  Several 3- or 4-inch "C" clamps
  2 sawhorses

Materials:
  96 l.f. 2x4 fir
  24 l.f. 2x6 fir
  180 l.f. 1x4 fir
  10' closet pole
  Box (50) 3/8" x 3" carriage bolts
  Box (50) 3/8" x 2-1/2" lag bolts
  2 lbs. 6d finishing nails
  1 gal. varnish

PLACE FOR PLANTS & SITTING

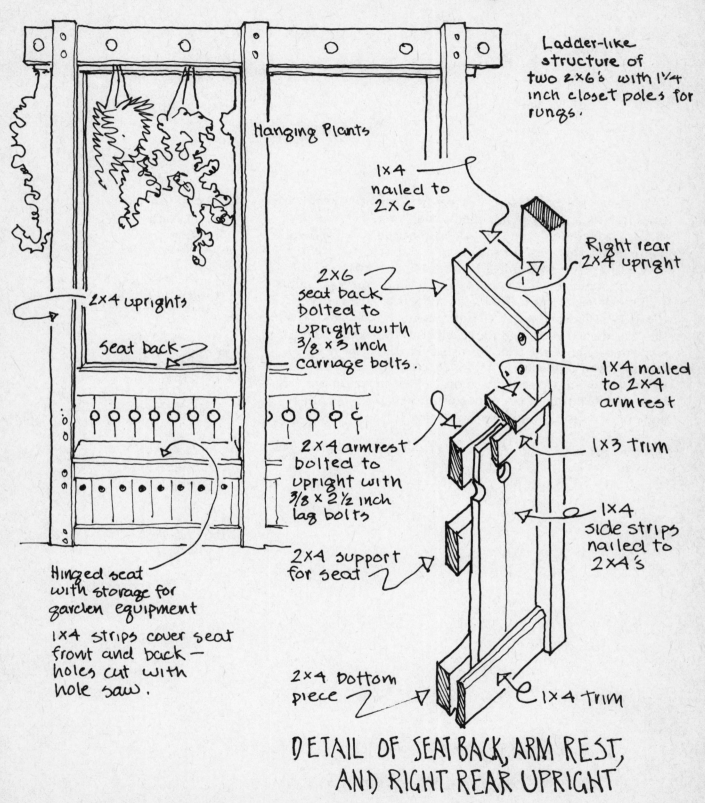

Ladder-like structure of two 2×6's with 1¼ inch closet poles for rungs.

Hanging Plants

1×4 nailed to 2×6

2×6 seat back bolted to upright with 3/8 × 3 inch carriage bolts.

Right rear 2×4 upright

2×4 uprights

Seat back

1×4 nailed to 2×4 armrest

1×3 trim

2×4 armrest bolted to upright with 3/8 × 2½ inch lag bolts

1×4 side strips nailed to 2×4's

2×4 support for seat

Hinged seat with storage for garden equipment

1×4 strips cover seat front and back — holes cut with hole saw.

2×4 bottom piece

1×4 trim

DETAIL OF SEAT BACK, ARM REST, AND RIGHT REAR UPRIGHT

PLAYHOUSE

This playhouse is scaled to the size of preschool children. It has three interior levels: ground, middle and tower. There are two slides, a ladder ramp, and two ladders. The walls are plywood — Baltic plywood is ideal for the purpose. Balusters support the roof. Long newel posts might be ladder sides. The pieces cut from the plywood with a sabre saw to form openings for doors could then be attached with hinges and used as the doors themselves. One method of finishing would be to apply a clear finish to the plywood, and warm bright paint to the other wooden parts, like the trims, balusters, balls and the newels. One idea is to divide the parts among a team of people who then paint them with two or three colors as they please. In this way each piece, while consistent in colors, differs from the others, and nobody has to do too much painting.

Skill Level: Advanced

Tools: Cabinetry Kit,
Sabre saw
Portable power saw

Materials:
5 sheets 4' x 6' x 1/2" Baltic plywood
2 sheets 4' x 8' x 3/4" birch-face plywood
70 l.f. 2x3 fir
7 1" x 36" dowels
6 balusters
2 newel posts, 6 ft. long
1 box (100) 2" no. 8 screws
1 box (100) 1-1/4" no. 6 screws
Hinges for doors

PLAYHOUSE

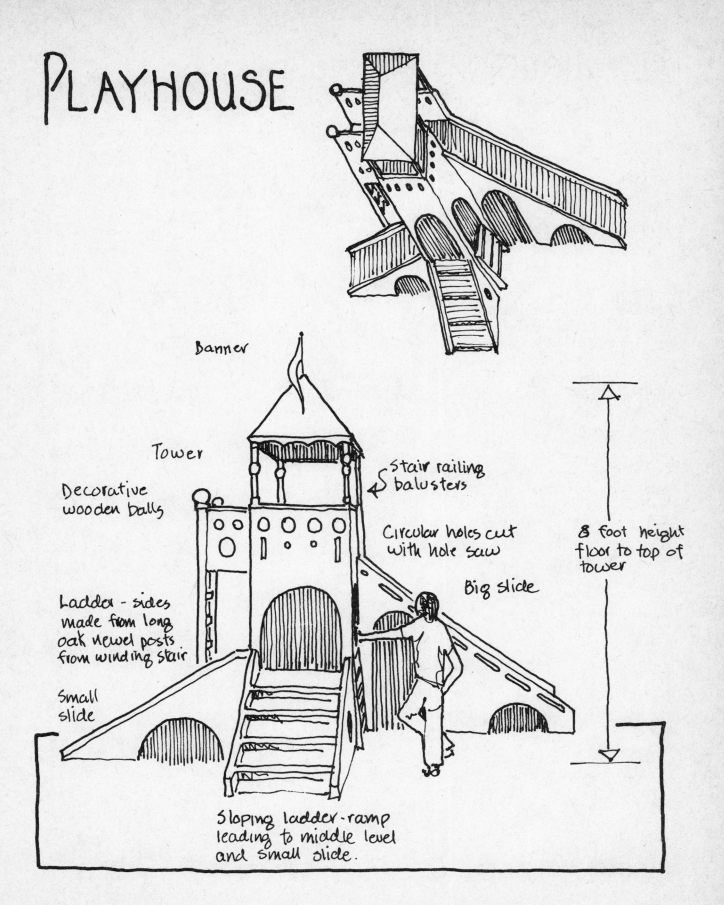

Banner

Tower

Decorative
wooden balls

Stair railing
balusters

Circular holes cut
with hole saw

Big slide

Ladder - sides
made from long
oak newel posts
from winding stair

Small
slide

8 foot height
floor to top of
tower

Sloping ladder-ramp
leading to middle level
and small slide.

AN ELEVATOR

Most elevators are pretty unimaginative places.

A few ideas for elevators are shown in this drawing. Most elevators have access hatches in the ceiling, which are for emergency use as well as maintenance. A window would reveal more about your elevator journey than a solid hatch. If the walls need painting, you could do another sun here. This is also an excellent location for a mosiac or a puzzle floor.

See also: Jan's Puzzle Floor, p. 74.
Mosaic Tiles, p. 72.

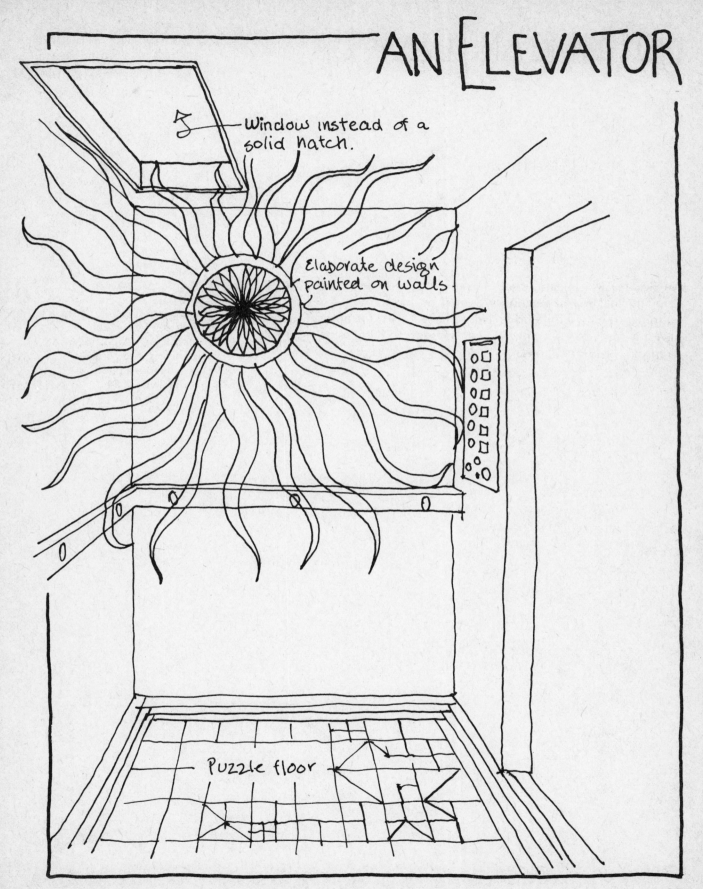

AN ELEVATOR

Window instead of a solid hatch.

Elaborate design painted on walls

Puzzle floor

OUTSIDE AN ELEVATOR

An elevator waiting area could be a place to wait for a friend, to stop and chat with a neighbor you met on the way into the building, to have a bulletin board, to have a corridor library, to have a garden, to put a special kind of floor, to hang some prints, paintings, or photographs.

See also: Corridor Library, p. 98.
Tack Wall, p. 8.
Jan's Puzzle Floor, p. 74.
A Corridor, p. 96.
A Place for Plants and Sitting, p. 88.
Window Shelves, p. 56 and 60.
Built-in Greenhouse, p. 62.
Rod and Brackets, p. 54.

Plants hanging from closet pole

Clip-on utility lamp

Books

Bulletin board

Elevator

Bench

Puzzle floor

A CORRIDOR

Corridors in apartment buildings are generally useless and even frightening alley-like places. Some things that can make them more useful and less frightening are pictures on walls, plants in windows, special windows instead of the standard ones, welcome mats. I have seen pictures on corridor walls near people's doorways, and they reveal something about the people who live there. This can help reduce the anonymity of neighbors. To make hanging and rehanging pictures easier, attach picture molding to the wall.

See also: Window in a Window, p. 48.
Movable Window Shelves, p. 60.
Built-in Greenhouse, p. 62.
Rod and Brackets, p. 54.
Corridor Library, p. 98.
Tack Wall, p. 8.
Peg and Shelf Rail, p. 10.

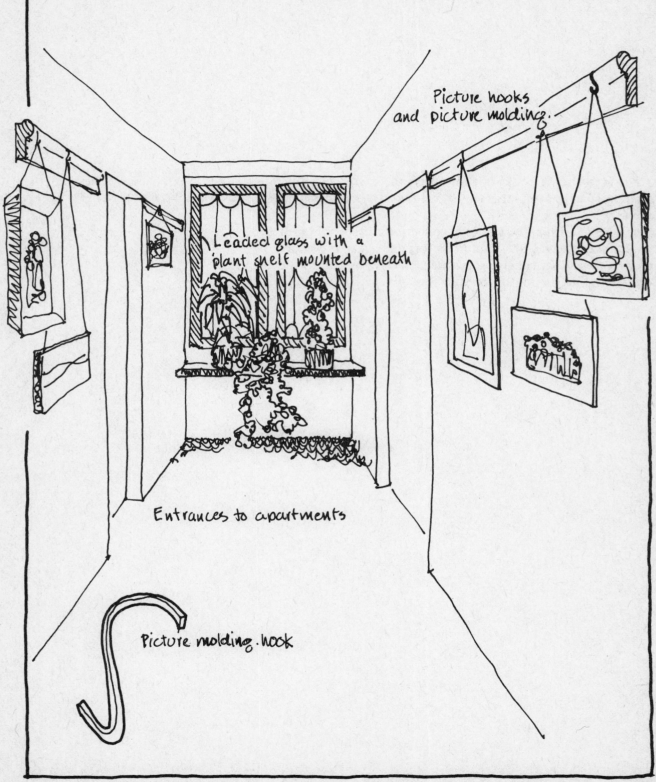

Picture hooks
and picture molding.

Leaded glass with a
plant shelf mounted beneath

Entrances to apartments

Picture molding. hook

Corridor Library

A friend put some books out for others to borrow and instead of disappearing, their numbers multiplied until a bookcase was needed.

Some apartment buildings have sections of corridors where a small library would fit. An old comfortable chair or even a large pillow or cushion will give someone a place to be comfortable while choosing a book to read.

See also: Adjustable Shelves, p. 14.
Canister and Spice Shelves, p. 116.

Old lamp

Book case

Bench

Large cushion

CORRIDOR LIBRARY

99

COMFORTABLE PLACE TO BATHE

Lights

Medicine cabinet

Mirror

Greenhouse built into window

Oak Trim

Band of colored tiles

Mirror

White ceramic tiles

Grab bar

Oak flooring used as wall surface

Old pedestal sink

Quarry tile floor

APPROXIMATELY JAN'S BATHROOM

Bathrooms

Why shouldn't a bathroom be a comfortable place to bathe, wake up, think, smile at yourself? Jan's bathroom is a comfortable room. The floor is clay-red quarry tile. The wainscoat, medicine cabinet, and trim are oak. The oak is oiled, giving it a warm satin gold finish. The tiles around the tub are 4-1/4-inch square white tiles except for two bands of small colored tiles (black, white, gray, and the clay red). Jan describes the medicine cabinet that he is building as also a kind of museum place for things he has collected. The cabinet is about five feet long and four feet high. Its doors and drawers are from salvaged pieces. The mirror beyond the toilet is the door to a linen storage cabinet built into the space where the pipes run at the head of the tub. The window has been converted into a greenhouse. (*See* p. 159)

CERAMIC TILES

This drawing shows walls of primarily simple square white tile, with a band of smaller colored tiles to relieve the monotony. Proper surface preparation and layout is the most important part of placing ceramic tiles on a wall. Follow the preparations detailed on p. 177. Before tiling, determine about how much you will be trimming from edge tiles. If the trimming is less than 1/4-inch, readjust your grid. Note also that the tiles aren't exactly the dimension they are supposed to be. (Try measuring a group of ten or so to determine the real dimensions.) Use wall-tile mastic and an appropriate trowel for spreading it. Read the instructions and cautions on the can. Renting a tile cutter from your dealer will save a lot of time and energy. Use tile nippers to trim the small tiles. If the tiles you're using do not have built-in spacers, you can use matchsticks.

Do one wall at a time. If you're sure to have perpendicular guidelines, you'll avoid a headache. Use white grout to fill the joints, and follow the same grouting procedure outlined for quarry tiles.

Skill Level: Basic

Tools: Tile cutter
Tile nippers
Mastic trowel
Rubber faced trowel

See also: General Preparations, p. 177.
Quarry Tiles, p. 70.

Materials:
Enough 4-1/4" x 4-1/4" white ceramic tile to cover the walls, and some extra
A few square feet of colored tiles
Wall-tile mastic
White grout

102

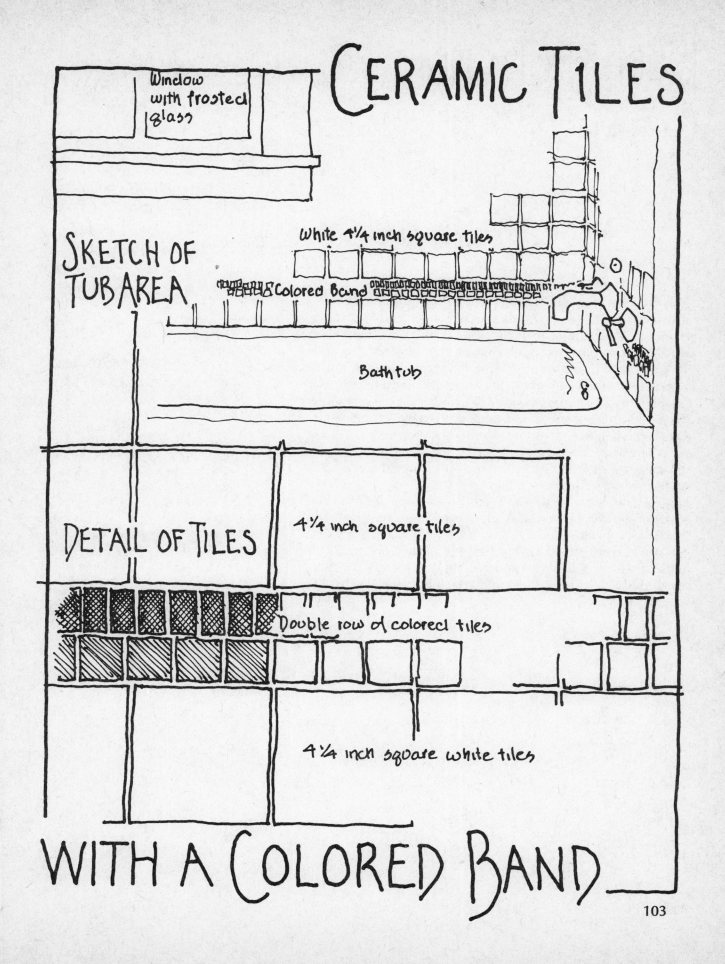

CERAMIC TILES

Window with frosted glass

SKETCH OF TUB AREA

White 4¼ inch square tiles

Colored Band

Bath tub

DETAIL OF TILES

4¼ inch square tiles

Double row of colored tiles

4¼ inch square white tiles

WITH A COLORED BAND

Bath Storage Cabinet

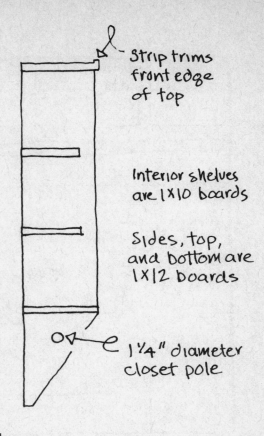

Strip trims front edge of top

Interior shelves are 1x10 boards

Sides, top, and bottom are 1x12 boards

1¼" diameter closet pole

CROSS-SECTION

This is a simple cabinet to construct. Eliminating the doors makes it still simpler. The doors shown are about 3-1/2 feet by 16 inches each, and made of fir. Unless you have other boards, no. 2 common pine is good enough for the project.

Cut all the pieces to size before doing any assembly. Be sure your edges are square and the boards are the right lengths. As drawn, you'll have to rip about 3/4 inch from each side piece. Use a ripsaw, sabre saw, or portable power saw. This job will be easier than you expect.

When all the pieces are properly sized, squared, and smoothed nail them together with 8d finishing nails. Hang the doors according to the instructions on p. 176.

The cabinet in the drawing rests on the top edge of the wainscoating or a strip of wood called a chairrail, which is commonly found in bathrooms.

This simplifies installation. Rest the cabinet on the rail and toenail it to the wall with 10d finishing nails. Or put a 1x3 strip across the back of the cabinet and attach it to the wall.

Skill Level: Basic (without the doors)
Advanced-basic (with doors)

Tools: Basic and ripsaw (without doors)
Basic and ripsaw, chisel, and mallet (with doors)

See also: Canister and Spice Shelves, p. 116.
Built-in Greenhouse, p. 62.
Hanging a Door, p. 176.
Entrance Trellis p. 78 (for toenailing).

Materials:
16 l.f. 1x12 boards
6 l.f. 1x10 boards
8 l.f. 1x3 strips
3 l.f. closet pole
3 l.f. trim

Bath Storage Cabinet

Fern

Doors from an old china cabinet

Cabinet rests on top edge of existing wainscoating

Towel bar made of 1¼" diameter closet pole

Bathtub

Mickey's Bathtub Garden

Mickey's garden was inspired by her bathtub-shower with its south-facing frosted glass window. Exposed to the humidity, the spray, the warmth, and the strong filtered light, plants will flourish.

The detail shows a window box that attaches to the window frame. The ends and sides are 1x8s; the bottom is a 1x6; 8d galvanized nails hold it together. The box should be about 1/4 inch shorter than the window opening is wide so that air can circulate and dry the space between the box and window stops. Screw the box to the window stops with 1-3/4-inch no. 8 screws, inserting washers between the box and stops as spacers.

The box could be replaced entirely with hanging plants. To hang a plant from the ceiling, find the floor joist above the ceiling plaster either by knocking or with a stud finder. Screw a large screwhook through the plaster into the joist. Such a hook will be two to three inches long and will need a pilot hole drilled into the joist.

Skill Level: Basic

Tools: Tape measure
Square
Hammer
Saw
Drill
Screwdriver

See also: Double-hung Window, p. 40.

Materials:
5 l.f. 1x8
20 in. 1x6
20 8d finishing nails
4 1-3/4" no. 8 screws
4 or more flat washers

MICKEY'S BATHTUB GARDEN

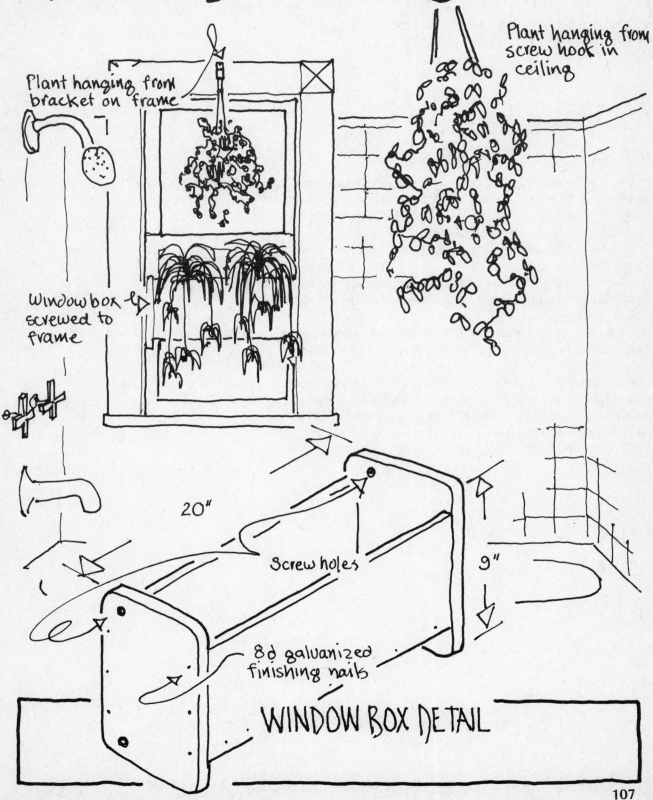

Plant hanging from bracket on frame

Plant hanging from screw hook in ceiling

Window box screwed to frame

20"

Screw holes

9"

8d galvanized finishing nails

WINDOW BOX DETAIL

Shelf and Concealed Lighting

It won't be too difficult to get more light where you need it, if there is already a light fixture on the wall. This sort of lighting is common in bathrooms and kitchens. The valance surrounding the fixtures acts as a shade. The space on top can be for storage or for plants such as ferns that like moisture and don't require strong light.

Remove the old fixture and cover the hole left by it with a cap purchased at a hardware store. Be sure to turn off the power before touching any wires.

A 1x6 should be wide enough for the top of the valance and a 1x4 wide enough for the front (depending on the light fixtures). I prefer the color of incandescent to fluorescent light and would use it if possible. Nail and glue the 1x6 to the 1x4 with 8d finishing nails. Support the valance on a 1x1 nailed to the walls. Be sure they are level. The new light fixtures can hook into the existing wiring. Caution: Be careful with the electrical work; get help unless you're sure of what you're doing.

Skill Level: Basic (some understanding of electrical recommended)

Tools: Basic Kit and wire cutters

Materials:
  1x6, as long as room is wide
  1x4, same length
  1x1, same length plus 8"
  1/4 lb. 8d finishing nails
  Glue

SHELF AND CONCEALED LIGHTING

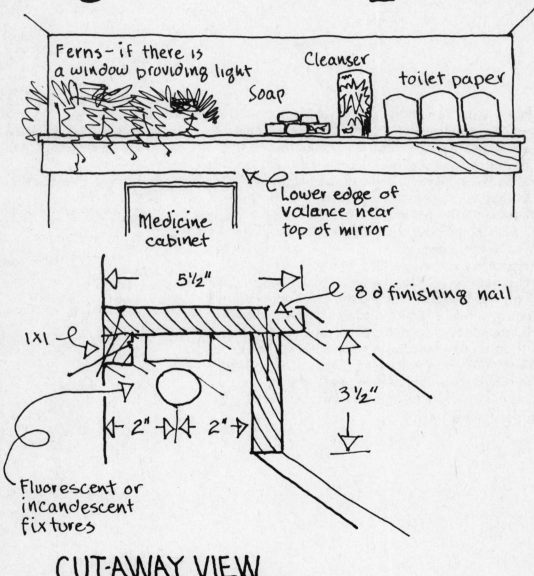

Ferns – if there is a window providing light

Cleanser

Soap

toilet paper

Medicine cabinet

Lower edge of valance near top of mirror

5½"

8 d finishing nail

1x1

3½"

2" 2"

Fluorescent or incandescent fixtures

CUT-AWAY VIEW

Lights and Medicine Chest

This medicine chest with its built-in lights fits around an existing mirror and medicine chest, supplying better light and needed extra space. In this situation, the bathtub is just to the left, the sink is below the mirror, and the toilet is below the right hand side. The shampoo is easy to reach while showering. Toothbrushes hang from nails or hooks in their own place. The nine-inch spacing between tall shelves is ideal for typical bathroom-type bottles like alcohol, peroxide, shampoo, hair rinse, bath oil. The other shelves are separated by six inches, but this could be reduced, depending upon what will sit on them.

The project is built of 1x4s for the verticals and horizontals, using 1/4-inch plywood for the back and the panels around the lights and electrical outlet. Begin by cutting the back and the hole in it to fit around the existing medicine cabinet. Butt the 1x4s and nail them together and to the back. Ideally, the electrical connections can tie into an existing fixture to be covered by the new cabinet. The light bulbs are 60-watt white globe bulbs. They cost more than standard bulbs, but they look better and last five times as long. (*See* p. 159)

Skill Level: Basic

Tools: Basic, and sabre saw or portable saw (to cut plywood)
Wire cutters

See also: Movable Window Shelves, p. 60.
Wiring from an Existing Fixture, p. 178.

Materials:
35 l.f. 1x4 common pine
1/4" x 4' x 4' A-B interior plywood
10 l.f. 1x1
1/2 lb. 8d finishing nails
Electrical wiring for three sockets and one receptacle

LIGHTS AND MEDICINE CHEST

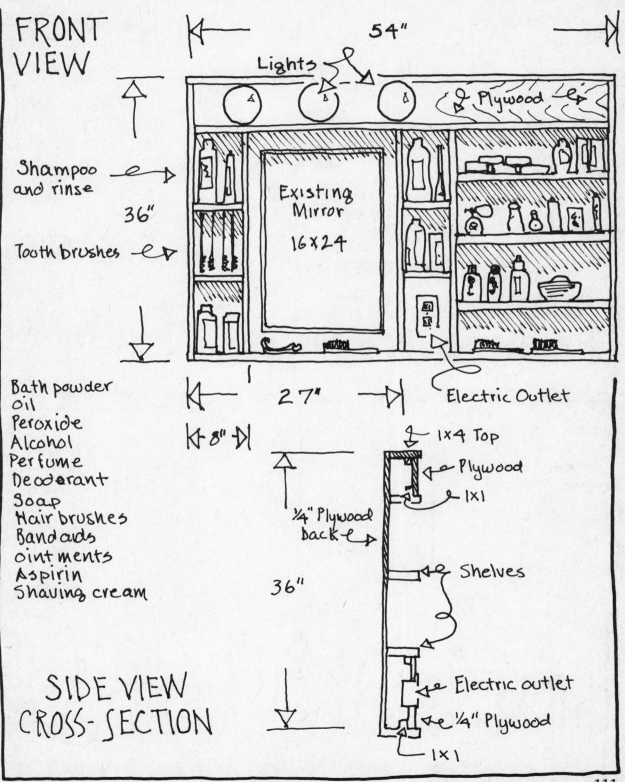

FRONT VIEW

54"

Lights

Plywood

Shampoo and rinse

36"

Tooth brushes

Existing Mirror 16 x 24

Electric Outlet

Bath powder
Oil
Peroxide
Alcohol
Perfume
Deodorant
Soap
Hair brushes
Band aids
ointments
Aspirin
Shaving cream

27"

8"

1x4 Top

Plywood

1x1

¼" Plywood back

Shelves

36"

Electric outlet

¼" Plywood

1x1

SIDE VIEW
CROSS-SECTION

SOME DIMENSIONS

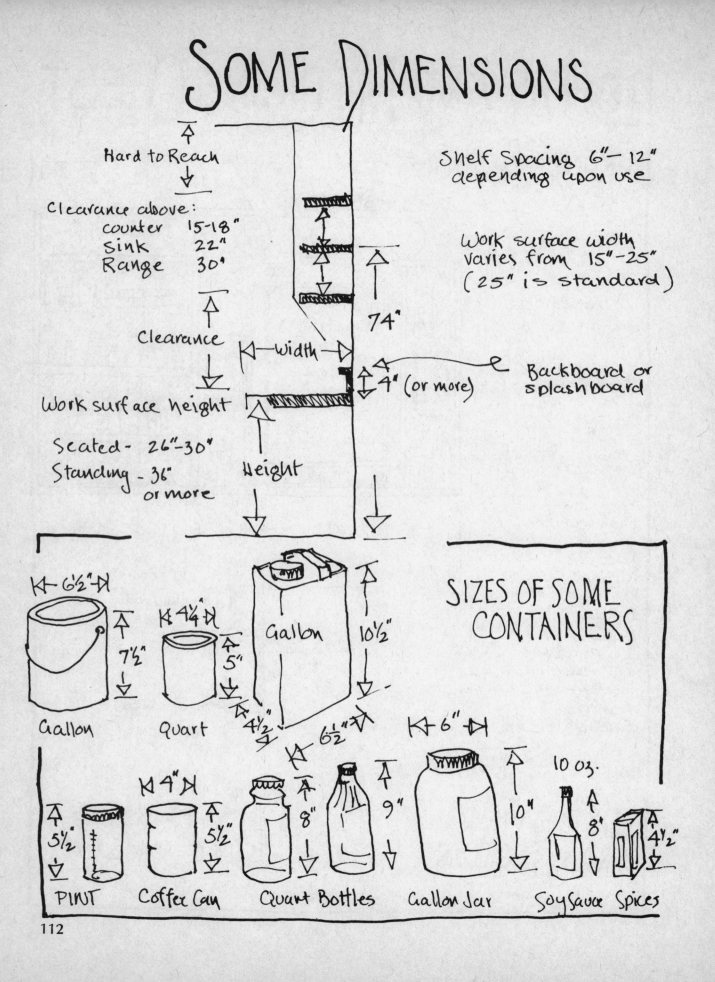

Hard to Reach

Clearance above:
- counter   15-18"
- Sink   22"
- Range   30"

Clearance

Work surface height

Seated - 26"-30"
Standing - 36" or more

Height

width

74"

4" (or more)

Shelf Spacing 6"—12" depending upon use

Work surface width varies from 15"-25" (25" is standard)

Backboard or splashboard

SIZES OF SOME CONTAINERS

6½"

7½"

Gallon

4¼"

5"

Quart

Gallon

10½"

4½"

6½"

5½"

PINT

4"

5½"

Coffee Can

8"

Quart Bottles

9"

6"

10"

Gallon Jar

10 oz.

8"

Soy Sauce

4½"

Spices

Kitchens and Other Work Areas

Mama's and Papa's kitchen was the biggest room in their house, with a pear tree outside always full of blue jays and sparrows. We ate breakfast there with the sun, the scrappy birds, the pear tree, and the vegetable garden beyond. They canned vegetables and put them up in the pantry, long and narrow with broad white shelves that extended to the ceiling. The dishes were on the left above the sink. The canned and dry goods were on the right. Everything had its place. There was also a closet in the kitchen were Papa kept assortments of brown paper bags, rubber bands, string, wire, nuts and bolts, tools, Band-Aids. The sink was twenty feet from the refrigerator. The children played under the breakfast table warmed by the stove and the sun in the window.

Margie and Peter's kitchen is barely larger than their bathroom. It is seven by eleven without any windows. They hired an architecture student to help them build counters and shelves. They built them of oak, some salvaged bowling alley, and old laboratory drawers. The oak glows in front of white walls as wide pantry-like shelves, but freer. The bowling alley is the counter top. They refinished the drawers and slid them into an oak base cabinet. Next they plan to paint a picture on the wall.

Both kitchens are functional. The first as a kitchen and major activity center because of its size, and the second as an efficient cooking space. The first has work and storage areas near the stove, refrigerator, and in the pantry. The second has work areas adjacent to sink, stove, and refrigerator. The second obeys the kitchen work-triangle law; the first does not.

Boxes and Hook Rail

Here are two ideas that can be independently implemented.

The hook rail is a 1x2 or salvaged molding, nailed to the wall with 8 or 10d finishing nails. Cup hooks come in a variety of sizes and screw into the rail easily by hand. The drawing shows six boxes: three soda cases and one Hildreth's Molasses Candy box for cookbooks and canisters, two fish boxes for spices. They sit on each other and the rail, and also are screwed to the wall. The screws can be small (1-1/4-inch no. 6) if the boxes rest on a rail, and won't even have to go into wall studs. If there is no rail, be careful to anchor the screws securely into the wall. A small utility lamp is clipped high in the center to light the work table. (*See* pp. 158, 161)

Skill Level: Simple

Tools: First Kit and drill

See also: Peg and Shelf Rail, p. 10.

Materials:
   1x2 or molding
   1 doz. cup hooks
   1 doz. 1-1/4" no. 6 screws
   8d finishing nails
   Boxes

BOXES AND HOOK RAIL

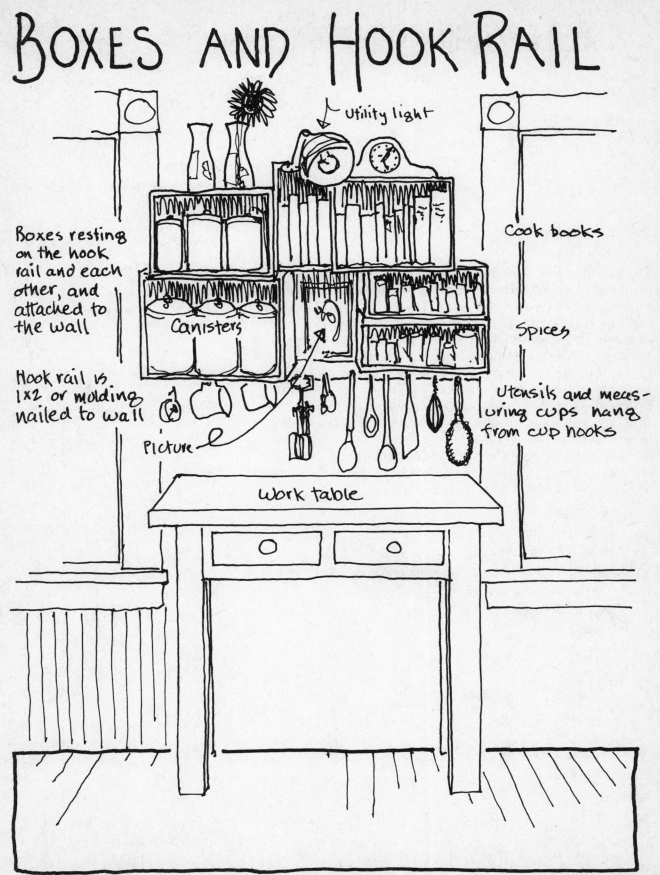

Utility light

Boxes resting on the hook rail and each other, and attached to the wall

Hook rail is 1×2 or molding nailed to wall

Cook books

Canisters

Spices

Picture

Utensils and measuring cups hang from cup hooks

Work table

Canister and Spice Shelves

Skill Level: Basic

Tools: Basic Kit and plane or Surform tools

See also: Bath Storage Cabinet, p. 104.

Materials:
30 l.f. 1x6 boards
20 l.f. shelf molding
4 l.f. closet pole
10 l.f. edge strip
1/4 lb. 8d finishing nails
1 qt. varnish

This set of shelves is constructed entirely of 1x6 boards and molding strips. The shelves fit between two doorways, and the three one-piece verticals rest on the top edge of the wainscoating that covers the bottom 3 feet of the wall. The lowest shelf is high enough to permit a work table beneath it. The highest shelf is low enough to be reached by persons who use the kitchen. The top shelf has a lip along its outer edge that prevents cutting boards, wooden bowls, or platters from sliding off when leaned against the wall. A refrigerator fits between two of the vertical supports, and beneath a shelf. There is also a towel bar made from a section of closet pole.

The shelves are built in place and hooked to the wall in the same way as bath storage cabinet, except the end verticals can be nailed to the door frames. (*See* p. 165)

Order of construction:

1. 76-inch top molding
2. three 39-inch verticals
3. two 48-inch and one 28-inch shelf with moldings
4. two small verticals
5. two small shelves
6. towel bar
7. varnish finish

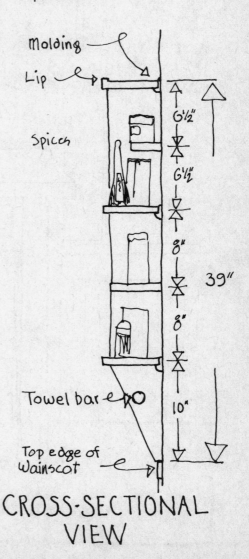

CROSS-SECTIONAL VIEW

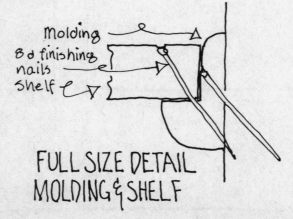

FULL SIZE DETAIL MOLDING & SHELF

Canister and Spice Shelves

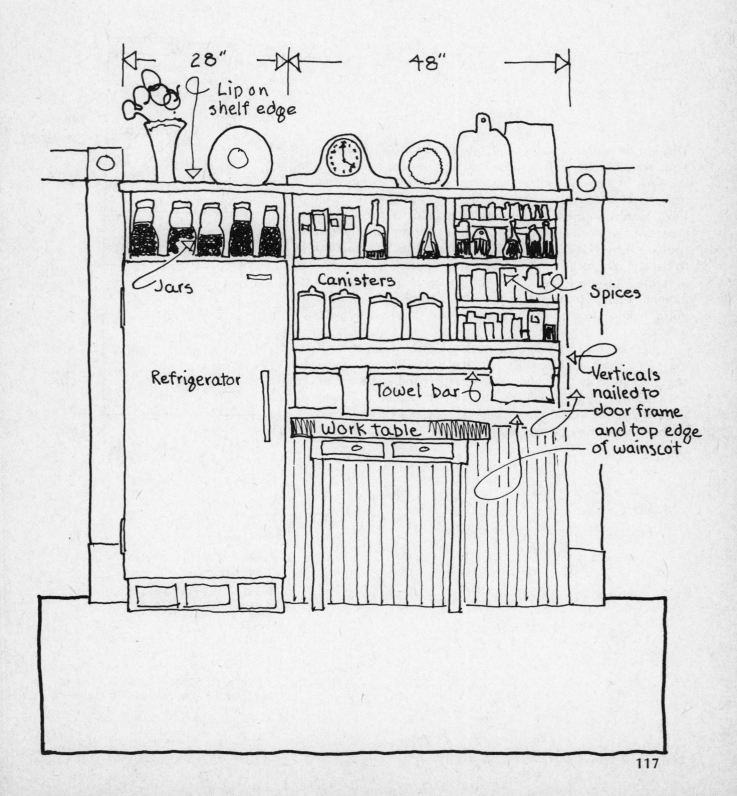

28"

48"

Lip on shelf edge

Jars

Canisters

Spices

Refrigerator

Towel bar

Verticals nailed to door frame and top edge of wainscot

Work table

LONG SHELVES

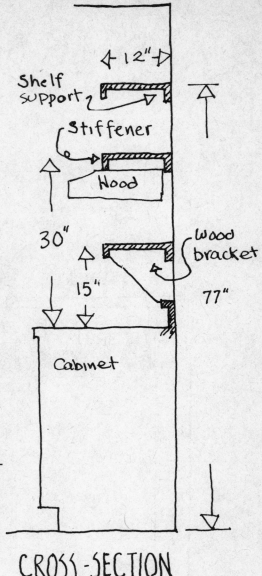

This is a simplified version of Margie and Peter's kitchen shelves. They wanted long shelves supported only on the ends and along the back. A simple 1x12 would warp along the unsupported front edge, so they attached a strip along that edge to stiffen it. Their span was nine feet and they used a strip 3/4 by 1-3/4 inches. A two-inch width would've been better. Since lumber comes 3/4 by 1-1/2 inches and 3/4 by 2-1/2 inches, you'd have to cut the two-inch width out of a wider board. Use a sabre or portable power saw. Use 8d finishing nails at six- to eight-inch intervals to attach the stiffener to the shelf. Watch out for knot holes. A knot hole on the bottom edge of the stiffener will weaken it.

Support the back and ends of the shelf on 1x2s or shelf molding. If the shelf is above the stove, there should be 30 inches between them. With 30 inches between shelf and stove and a foot between the top two shelves, the top shelf will be at 77 inches, a little higher than ideal (74 inches). Margie and Peter had no problem with the extra reach.

CROSS-SECTION

Skill Level: Basic

Tools: Basic Kit and sabre saw or portable power saw

See also: Canister and Spice Shelf, p. 116. Molly Bolts, p. 174.

Materials:
3 1x12s, 9' long (shelves and brackets)
1 1x8, 9' long (stiffeners)
3 1x2s, 10' long (shelf supports)
1/2 lb. 8d finishing nails
1/2 lb. 10d finishing nails or Molly bolts
Wood glue

LONG SHELVES

Range hood

Counter

Range

119

Fold-down Work Space

This fold-down work surface is made of four main pieces: the back board, the work surface itself and two supporting legs. Its precise construction depends upon your level of ability, the tools you have on hand, your budget, and the materials available. An expensive work surface of maple butcher block could be purchased or fabricated easily in a well-equipped wood shop. A section salvaged from an old desk top, or plywood covered with an industrial grade of linoleum and edged with strips of soft- or hardwood are two alternatives to the more expensive butcher block.

Secure the work surface to the backboard with piano hinges. Screw the backboard to the wall. Use 2-1/2 inch no. 10 or larger screws in a wood stud wall, or Molly bolts in a metal stud wall. Brass round-head screws in conjunction with washers have an appealing finished appearance.

Attach the support legs to 1x2s with hinges and secure them to the wall in the same manner as the back board. Make the legs from plywood or a wide board.

Skill Level: Basic

Tools: Basic Kit

See also: Wood Stud Wall, p. 2. Hinges, p. 174.

Materials:
- 16 l.f. 1x2
- 4-1/2 l.f. 1x6
- 1/2" x 13-1/2" x 52-1/2" plywood
- 13-1/2 x 52-1/2" linoleum or vinyl flooring
- 14 2-1/2" no. 10 screws
- 6-1/2 ft. piano hinge

FOLD-DOWN WORK SPACE

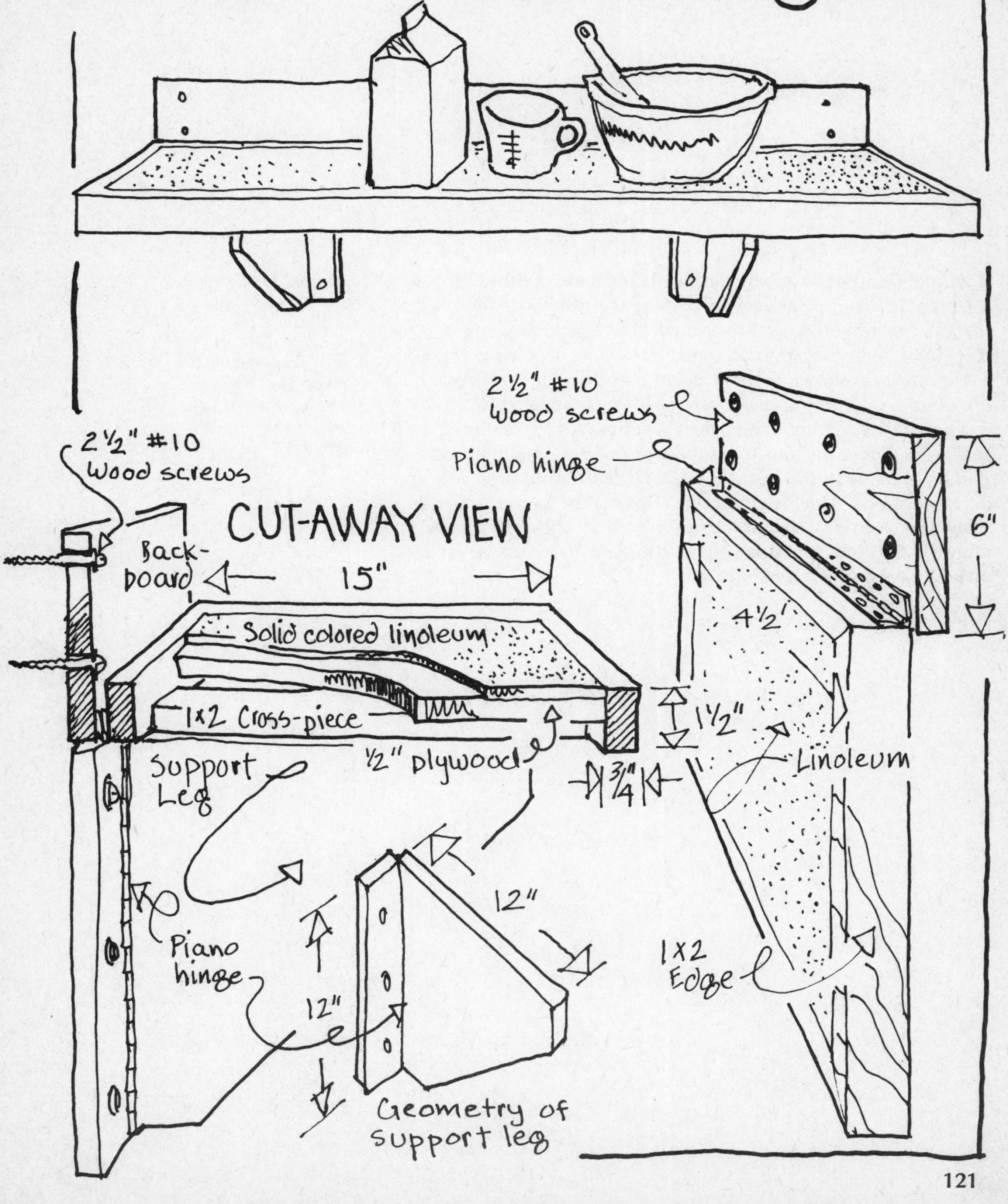

CUT-AWAY VIEW

2½" #10 wood screws

Piano hinge

2½" #10 Wood screws

6"

4½"

Back-board

15"

Solid colored linoleum

1×2 Cross-piece

½" plywood

1½"

¾"

Linoleum

Support Leg

Piano hinge

12"

12"

1×2 Edge

Geometry of support leg

A Pantry

Most older houses have pantries, while most new houses do not. A pantry has the advantages of keeping clutter out of the kitchen, eliminating the need for wall cabinets, and allowing nearly everything to be stored in one small area. The drawing is a collection of ideas shown in more detail on other pages. There are three types of shelving: a slat shelf, shelves supported by moldings and a vertical board, and shelves supported by moldings and posts. There are bins for storage of potatoes and onions. The space beneath the counter was adapted for old desk and bureau drawers. The moldings that support the back edge of the shelves on the right extend for hooks to hold cups, pots, pans, utensils, a broom, a dustpan. Also, the presence of a step ladder makes high shelves accessible.

See also: Slat Shelves, p. 124.
Canister and Spice Shelves, p. 116.
Bins, p. 126.
Base Cabinet, p. 128.
Drawers and Glides, p. 132.
Hanging Doors, p. 176.
Hook Rail, p. 114.

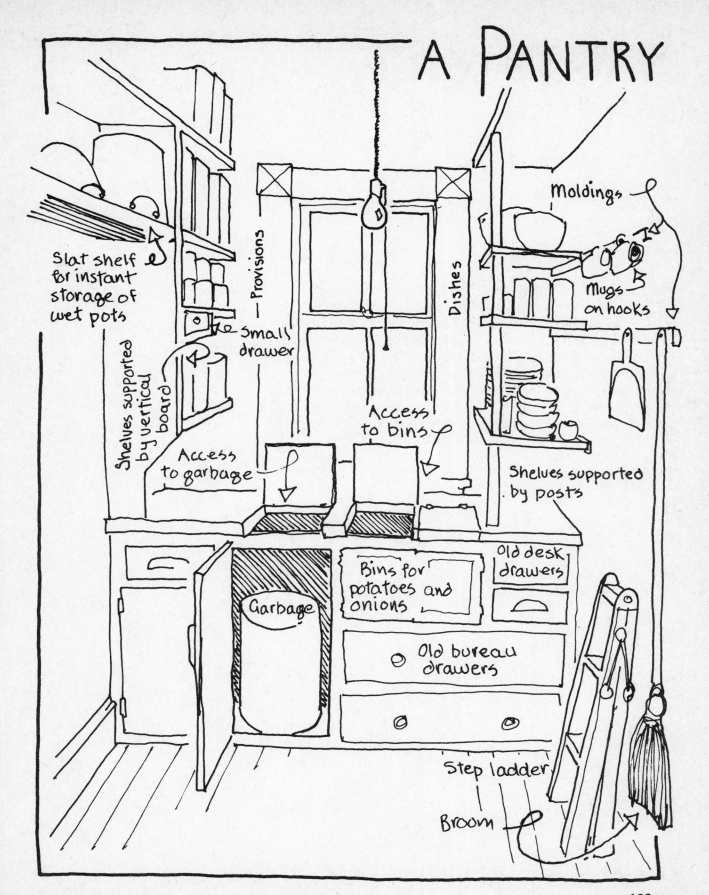

A PANTRY

Slat shelf for instant storage of wet pots

Shelves supported by vertical board

Provisions

Dishes

moldings

Mugs on hooks

Small drawer

Access to garbage

Access to bins

Shelves supported by posts

Garbage

Bins for potatoes and onions

Old desk drawers

Old bureau drawers

Step ladder

Broom

Slat Shelves

The slats used for these shelves are 1x2s, also called *strapping*. Strapping normally serves for rough carpentry and packing crates. You can buy it, but you can also find it discarded at construction sites and places that use large packing cases. You can also buy better-grade lumber, such as clear pine, fir, or redwood, to make first-class slat shelves. Use varnish, polyurethane, or enamel paint for a finish. All saw cuts must be square where pieces join. If you use the dowel or crosspiece on the bottom method, you can cut the shelf to length after you put it together.

Skill Level: Basic

Tools: Basic Kit

See also: A Pantry, p. 122.

Materials:
  1x2 strapping
  1/4 lb. 8d finishing nails
  3/4" dowel

SLAT SHELVES

Cooking vessels drying on a slat shelf

THREE WAYS TO CONSTRUCT SLAT SHELVES

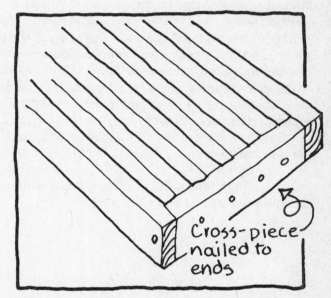

Cross-piece nailed to ends

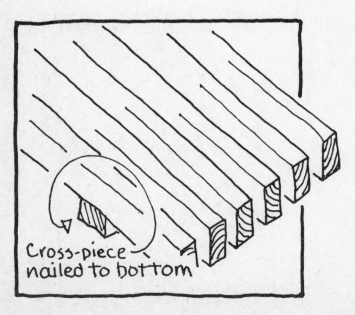

Cross-piece nailed to bottom

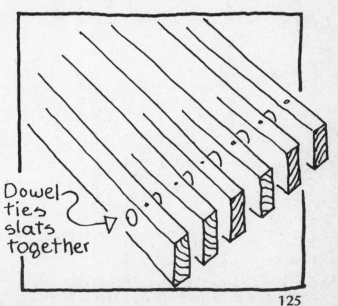

Dowel ties slats together

Potato and Onion Bin

There are two parts to this project, the bin itself and the lids cut out of and hinged to the counter. The latter may be the most difficult.

Half-inch plywood is a good material for the bin. Cut the pieces, and drill the ventilation holes. Be sure the parts fit properly before nailing them together. A sabre saw will cut plywood quickly and easily. Use a fine-toothed blade for a smooth cut. A Surform tool or a plane is helpful in making minor adjustments to the sizes of parts.

Cut the lid openings with a sabre saw. Notice that the inside corners can be rounded for ease in cutting. Follow the hinging directions on p. 174.

Attach the bin to the counter bottom with 3/4-inch no. 8 flat-head screws and angle brackets.

Skill Level: Difficult side of Basic

Tools: Basic Kit and sabre saw
   Sabre saw
   Combination square
   Chisel
   Mallet

Materials: (see sketch)
   2 side pieces
   1 divider (or more)
   1 back
   1 front
   1 bottom
   1/4 lb. 6d finishing nails
   8 3/4" no. 8 flat head screws
   4 angle brackets
   4 hinges

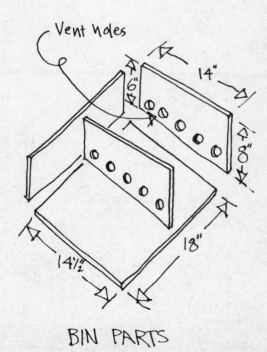

Vent holes

14"

6"

8"

14½"

18"

BIN PARTS

POTATO AND ONION BIN

EXPLODED VIEW

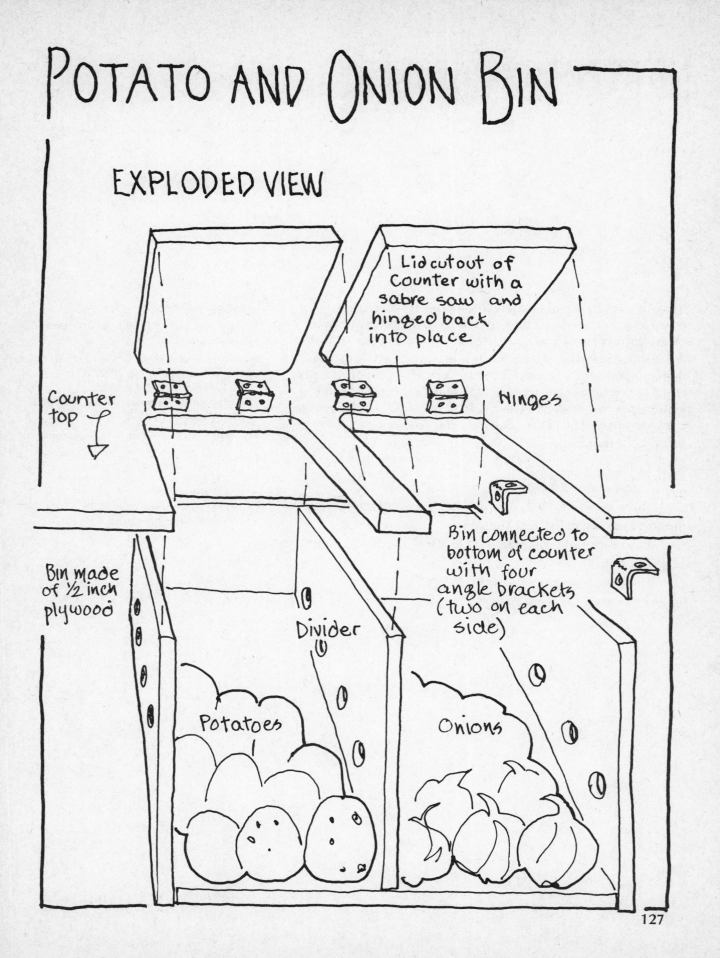

Lid cut out of Counter with a sabre saw and hinged back into place

Counter top ↓

Hinges

Bin made of ½ inch plywood

Divider

Bin connected to bottom of counter with four angle brackets (two on each side)

Potatoes

Onions

New Base Cabinet

You will need to replace a metal base cabinet when it is too rusted to scrape and repaint. Old desk and laboratory drawers are the correct size for kitchen use. The space directly in front of the sink is usually wasted, but it is an ideal place for soap, sponges, scouring pads, etc. The space below the sink is usually left as cabinet, but another idea is to build a second box, containing drawers and cabinet space, that will slide out if there is a need to service the pipes. (See pp. 160, 161)

Steps in Building:

1. Collect doors and drawers.

2. Plan cabinet around sink, doors, and drawers.

3. Build the simple box base cabinet shown in the sketch, using glue and 8d nails; next the pedestal, using 10d nails.

4. Disconnect old sink, remove old base, install new, and reconnect sink.

5. Build cabinet front.

Take your time and be inventive.

Skill Level: Advanced

Tools: Cabinetry Kit and portable power saw or sabre saw

See also: Swing-Down Drawer, p. 130.
Drawers and Glides, p. 132.
Built-in Greenhouse, p. 62.
Bath Storage Cabinet, p. 104.
Hanging Doors, p. 176.

Materials: (for base box 4-1/2 feet long)
2 sheets 3/4'' x 4' x 8' A-B interior plywood, or better
12 l.f. 2x4s
Wood glue
1/2 lb. 8d finishing nails
A few 10d finishing nails

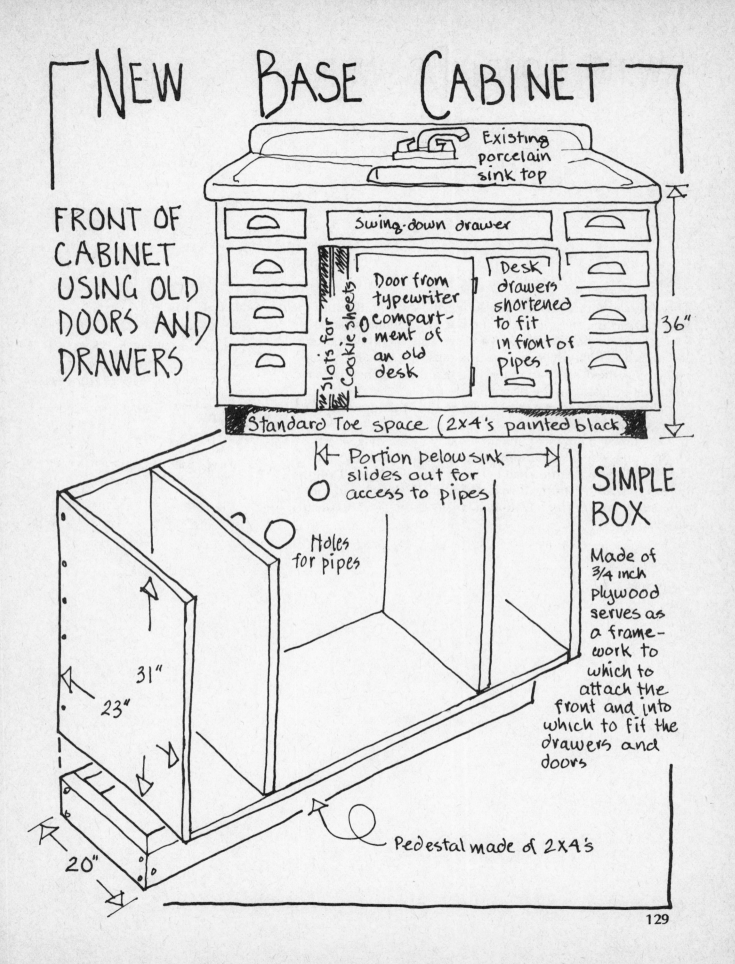

New Base Cabinet

FRONT OF
CABINET
USING OLD
DOORS AND
DRAWERS

Existing porcelain sink top

Swing-down drawer

Slots for Cookie sheets

Door from typewriter compartment of an old desk

Desk drawers shortened to fit in front of pipes

36"

Standard Toe space (2×4's painted black)

Portion below sink slides out for access to pipes

Holes for pipes

SIMPLE BOX

Made of 3/4 inch plywood serves as a frame-work to which to attach the front and into which to fit the drawers and doors

31"

23"

Pedestal made of 2×4's

20"

Swing-Down Drawer

This project requires careful measuring and cutting. Because the wood is thin and the parts small, minor errors will appear large. The drawer is a box attached to a front. Use thin plywood or a thin board to build the box. The box must not only be narrow enough for the designated space, but also the diagonal on the end must be less than the height.

The front should match or relate to the other drawers and doors in the cabinet.

The dowel holes must line up directly or the hinge mechanism won't work. Measure the hole locations carefully and make indentations with a nail before drilling the holes. Drill the hole in the cabinet front the exact size of the dowel, and the hole in the drawer front 1/16-inch larger. Use 1/4- or 3/8-inch dowels.

Skill Level: Basic

Tools: Basic Kit

See also: Base Cabinet, p. 128.

Materials:
Thin plywood or lumber 1/2" or less
Drawer front
1/4" or 3/8" dowel
Knob
4 1-1/2" no. 8 screws
2 3/4" screws
4d or 6d nails
Glue

SWING-DOWN DRAWER

Front edge of counter top

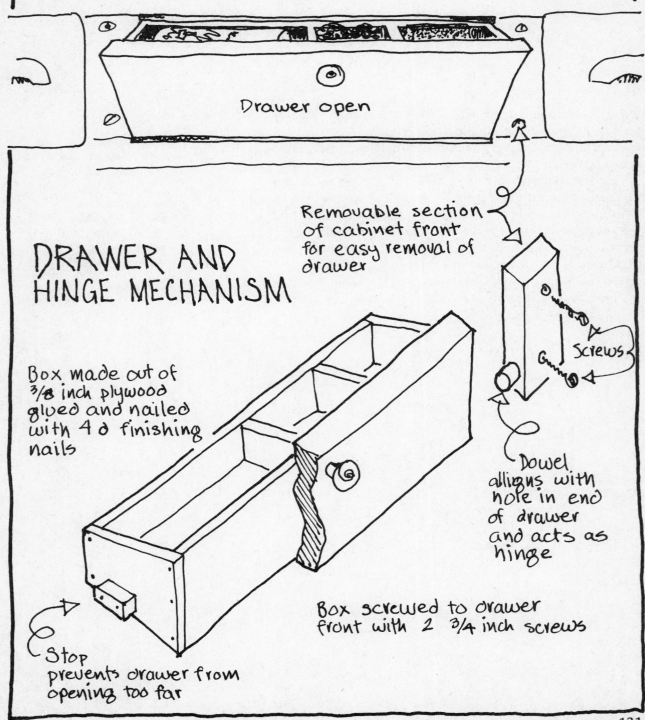

Drawer open

DRAWER AND HINGE MECHANISM

Removable section of cabinet front for easy removal of drawer

Screws

Box made out of 3/8 inch plywood glued and nailed with 4 d finishing nails

Dowel alligns with hole in end of drawer and acts as hinge

Box screwed to drawer front with 2 3/4 inch screws

Stop prevents drawer from opening too far

131

Two Drawers and Glides

If you are building kitchen base cabinets or a desk, these sketches show two common and simple drawer details. As noted earlier, old desk and lab drawers are ideal for kitchens. A deep drawer is a good potato bin; a shallow drawer is perfect for utensils.

The simplest drawer glide is a shelf. A refined method replaces the shelf with two strips of wood that support the drawer bottom, or grooves in the sides. Maple is a good material for glides because it is hard and won't wear down quickly. Strips that run in grooves on drawer sides will prevent the drawer from tilting when it is pulled beyond its center of gravity.

Attach the glide strips to the sides of the cabinet with screws and glue. Be sure they are level and at the same height. (*See* pp. 160, 161)

Skill Level: Basic

Tools: Basic Kit

See also: New Base Cabinet, p. 128. Built-in Storage Wall, p. 16.

Materials: (for each drawer)
2 glides as long as drawer
4 no. 6 or no. 8 wood screws (length determined by situation)
Wood glue

TWO DRAWERS AND GLIDES

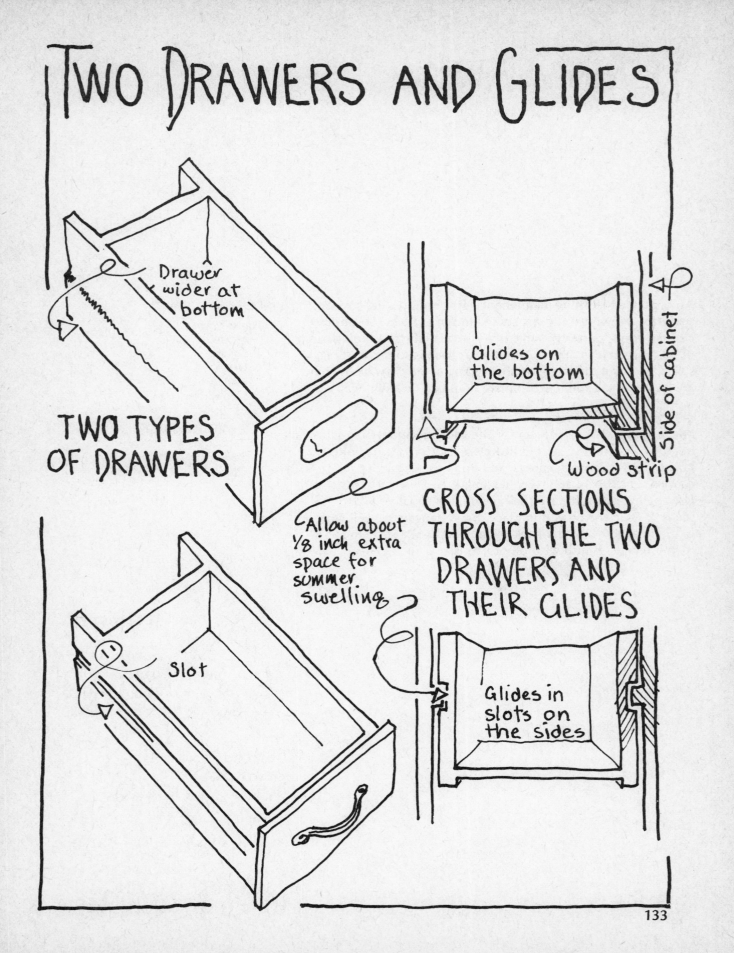

Drawer wider at bottom

TWO TYPES OF DRAWERS

Glides on the bottom

Side of cabinet

Wood strip

Allow about 1/8 inch extra space for summer swelling

Slot

CROSS SECTIONS THROUGH THE TWO DRAWERS AND THEIR GLIDES

Glides in slots on the sides

Sewing Area

An organized clothing maintenance area requires little space: space for a sewing machine, some kind of storage for fabrics, clothes, tools, patterns, some place to cut fabric (a dining room or kitchen table is okay). An old wardrobe is suitable storage space, especially if there are shelves and some drawers. If there are two doors, a full-length mirror could go on each one.

Spool and Tool Board

Mickey suggested the design for the tool and spool board, an oak board with carefully spaced dowels attached to it. It holds a tailor's curve, scissors, spools, and bobbins, Use 1/8- or 3/16-inch dowels. Cut the dowels to equal length (1-1/4 to 1-1/2 inches). Use the jig shown to drill the hole depths equally (1/2 to 5/8 inches). Glue the dowels in place. Brass hangers go well with oak. These screw to the back of the board. Space them at 16-inch intervals. Finish with oil or varnish.

Skill Level: Basic

Tools: Saw
  Measure
  Square
  Drill
  Mallet
  Screwdriver

Materials:
  7 x 21" board (oak)
  2 1/8" dowels
  2 brass hangers
  Glue

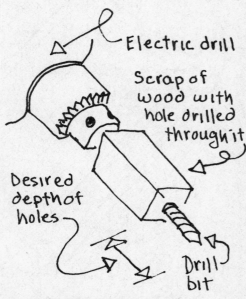

Electric drill

Scrap of wood with hole drilled through it

Desired depth of holes

Drill bit

JIG FOR DRILLING HOLES OF EQUAL DEPTH

SEWING AREA

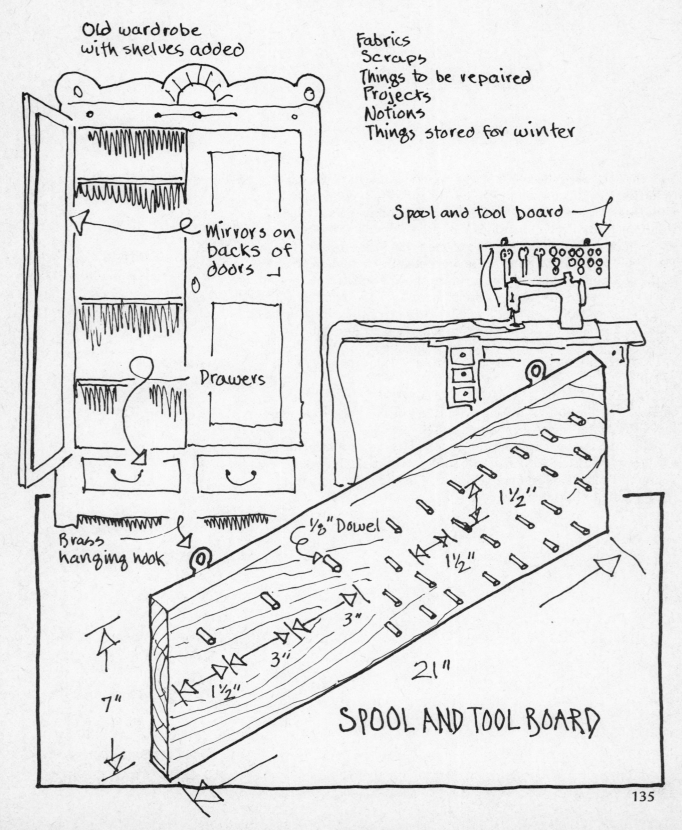

Old wardrobe with shelves added

Fabrics
Scraps
Things to be repaired
Projects
Notions
Things stored for winter

Mirrors on backs of doors

Drawers

Spool and tool board

Brass hanging hook

1/8" Dowel

1½"

1½"

3"

3"

1½"

7"

21"

SPOOL AND TOOL BOARD

Sawhorse Construction

This is the classic carpenter's sawhorse with a few dimensional modifications, so that a pair can be legs for a study-work-play table. Standard sawhorses have 24-inch legs and 3-1/2- to 4-foot length instead of the dimensions indicated.

You can use a framing square to determine the angle cuts on the legs. The angles give the horse more stability and strength. With the framing square in the position shown, draw a line for the top cut. Turn the square around and draw a line parallel to, and 25 inches from, the first line. Similarly mark the edges for the side angle (both cuts will be compound angles), but this time, use 5-5/8 inches and 24 inches as the points on the square. The cut looks frightening, but just be careful to begin following both cut lines.

Trace a leg on the 2x4 to mark the cuts for the gains. Cut the sides of the gain so that the leg will just fit in and not wiggle. Remove the center of the gain with a chisel.

Eight-penny *box* nails are the appropriate nails for attaching the legs and gussets. (Box nails are similar to but slimmer than common nails.) Glue and nail all joints. Cut the plywood gussets with a sabre or portable power saw.

Skill Level: Basic

Tools: Framing square
Crosscut saw
Hammer
Chisel
Sabre or portable power saw (optional)

See also: Sawhorse Worktable, p. 138.

Materials:
6 l.f. 2x4 — a straight piece, preferably without knots
20 l.f. 1x4 clear pine
3/8" x 16" x 36" plywood
1/2 lb. 8d boxnails
Wood glue

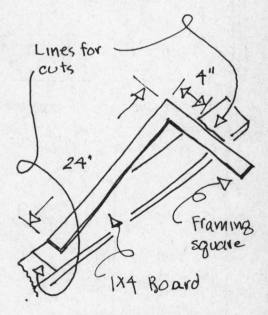

Using a framing square to mark for cuts on legs

Sawhorse Construction

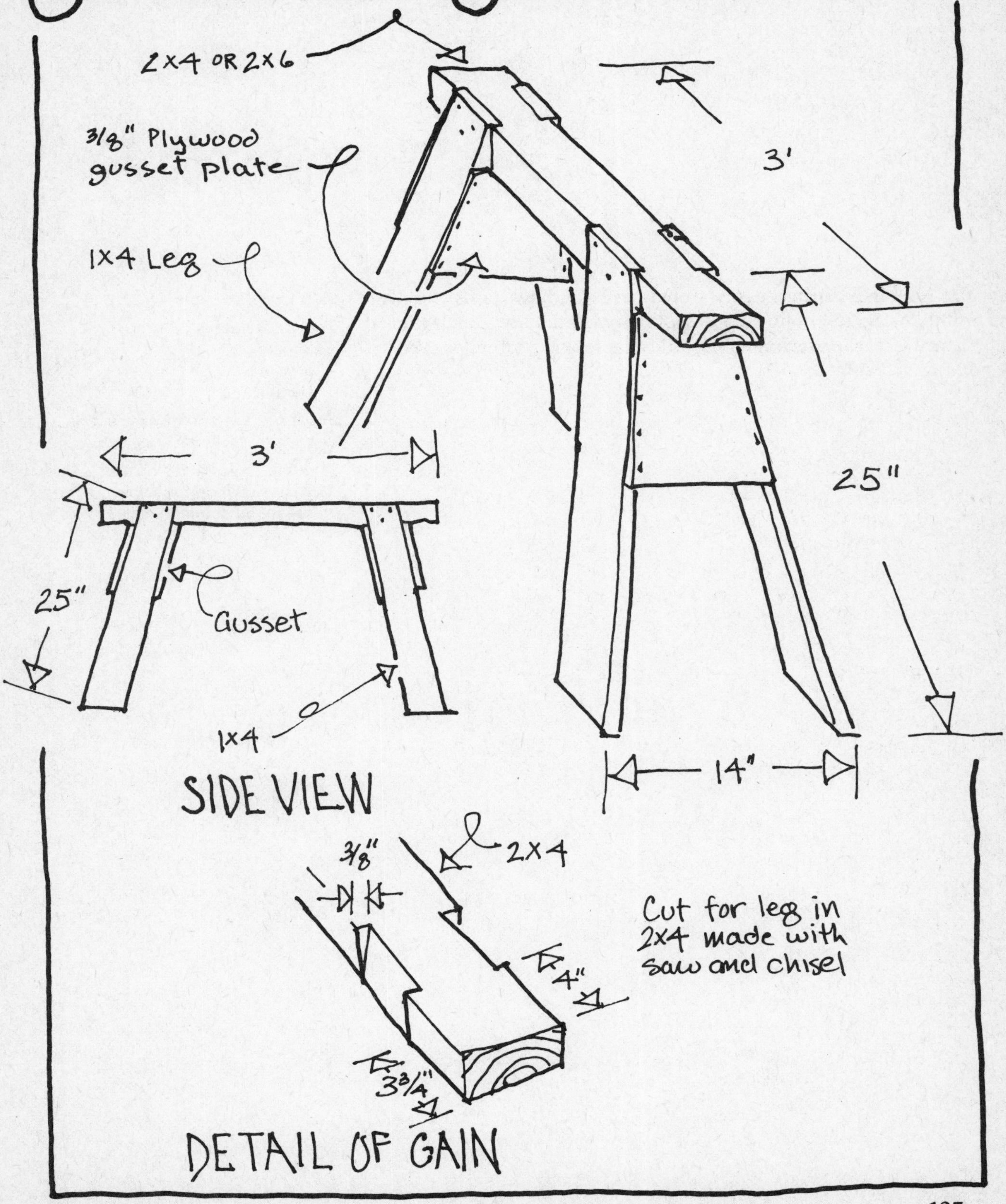

2x4 or 2x6

3/8" Plywood
gusset plate

1x4 Leg

3'

25"

3'

25"

Gusset

1x4

14"

SIDE VIEW

3/8"

2x4

4"

3 3/4"

Cut for leg in
2x4 made with
saw and chisel

DETAIL OF GAIN

Sawhorse Worktable

This is an inexpensive, easily stored table. Lumber yards and ply-wood dealers sell hollow-core doors, or you can use 2-inch thick planks. Great for sewing table, study table, kids' table, or even dining.

Skill Level: Simple

Tools: Measure
Square
Saw
Hammer

See also: Sawhorse Construction, p. 136.

Materials:
3 8-ft. 2x4s (cheap quality is fine)
2 pairs sawhorse brackets
1/4 lb. 6d common nails

SAWHORSE WORKTABLE

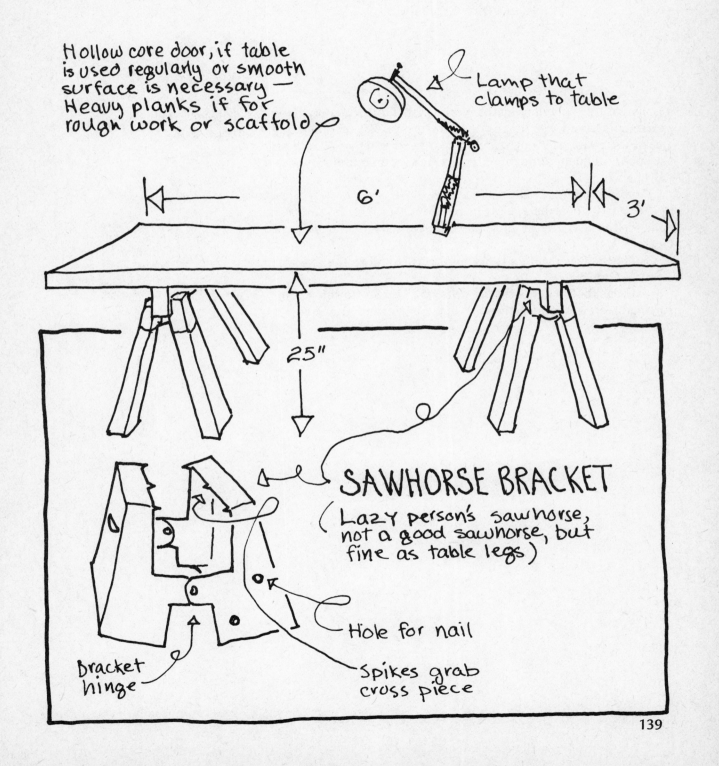

Hollow core door, if table is used regularly or smooth surface is necessary — Heavy planks if for rough work or scaffold

Lamp that clamps to table

6'

3'

25"

SAWHORSE BRACKET

(Lazy person's sawhorse, not a good sawhorse, but fine as table legs)

Hole for nail

bracket hinge

Spikes grab cross piece

WORKBENCH

This is a sturdy, uncomplicated workbench. Unfortunately, few apartments have space for this kind of furniture. There may be a cellar or a garage, though, and in a large building you could ask the superintendent about supplying space for a community workbench.

To build the top, nail 2x4s to three cleats; first the 2x4 cleat in the center, then the 2x6 cleats near the ends. Use 8d common nails for the center cleat and 12d common nails for the end cleats.

Build the legs from 2x4s bolted together and to the 2x6 cleats as shown.

The backboard and shelf are optional. Use 8d finishing nails for them. Drawers and shelves can also be installed at a later date.

Skill Level: Basic

Tools: Basic

Materials:
- 36 l.f. 2x6
- 24 l.f. 2x4
- 8 l.f. 1x8
- 7 l.f. 1x4
- 1/2" x 15" x 5' plywood
- 1/2 lb. 8d common nails
- 1/2 lb. 12d common nails
- 1/2 lb. 8d finishing nails
- 12 3/8" x 3-1/2" carriage bolts
- 4 3/8" x 4-1/2" carriage bolts

WORKBENCH

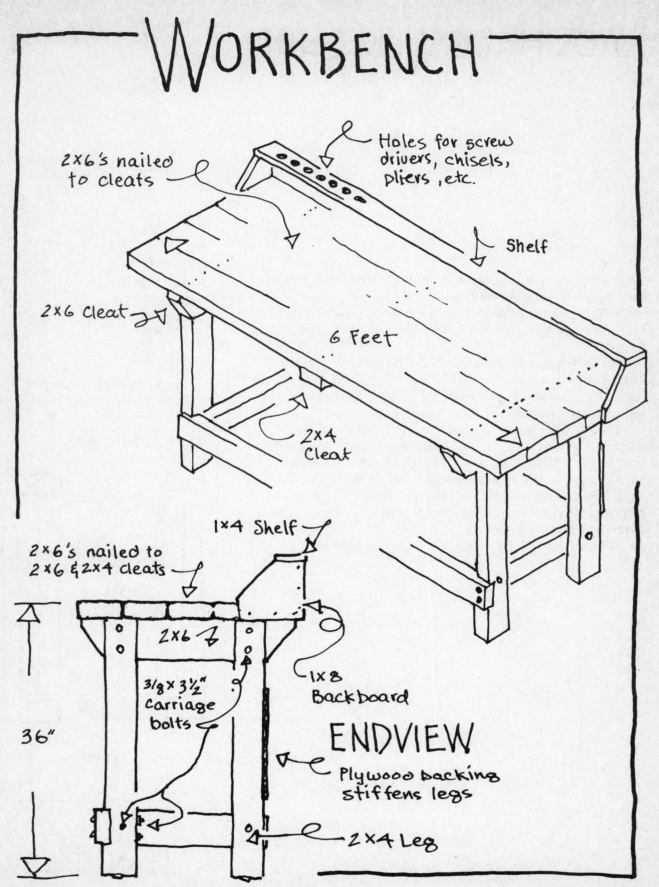

Holes for screw drivers, chisels, pliers, etc.

2x6's nailed to cleats

Shelf

2x6 Cleat

6 Feet

2x4 Cleat

2x6's nailed to 2x6 & 2x4 cleats

1x4 Shelf

2x6

3/8 x 3½" Carriage bolts

1x8 Backboard

36"

ENDVIEW

Plywood backing stiffens legs

2x4 Leg

BACK HALL WORKSHOP

A back hall going, for instance, from the kitchen to a porch or back yard, is a good location for tool storage or a small work space. The amount of work that can be done in a four- or five-foot space is limited, but this area might serve handily for small projects.

My back hall is evolving into something like the sketch. A 2x12 is the work surface (make it wider, if possible), 1x12s are for shelves beneath it, wall space for hanging tools, and a 1x6 for additional storage just above head height.

The work surface is supported by 1x3s nailed to the wall, and by two vertical 1x12s. The 1x12 shelves are supported at their ends by 1x3s. A piece of 1/2-inch plywood or 1/4-inch peg board simplifies the organization of tools on the wall.

If you are not familiar with the jar trick, it's a good use for empties that you hate to throw away. Just nail or screw the lid to the underside of a shelf.

A good mobile light source and a vise are both handy.

Skill Level: Basic

Tools: Basic Kit

Materials:
- 6 l.f. 1x6
- 5 l.f. 2x12
- 24 l.f. 1x12
- 28 l.f. 1x3
- 4 l.f. 1x4
- 1 lb. 8d finishing nails
- 1/2 lb. 10d finishing nails

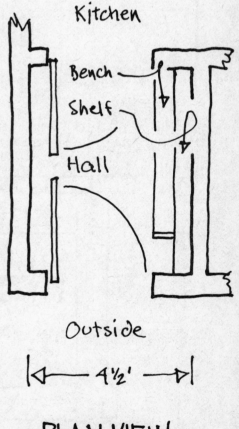

Kitchen

Bench

Shelf

Hall

Outside

|← 4½' →|

PLAN VIEW

Back Hall Workshop

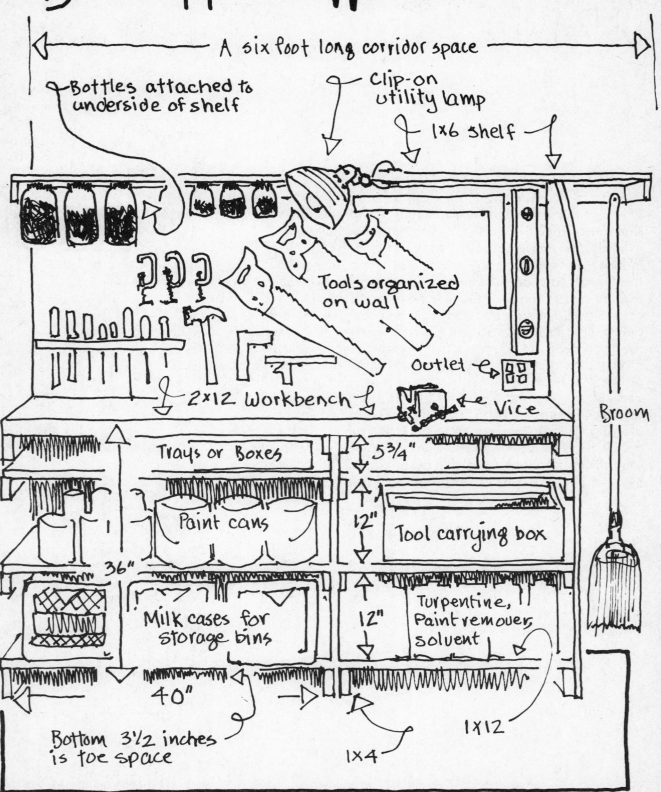

A six foot long corridor space

Bottles attached to underside of shelf

Clip-on utility lamp

1x6 shelf

Tools organized on wall

Outlet

2x12 Workbench

Vice

Broom

Trays or Boxes

5¾"

Paint cans

12"

Tool carrying box

36"

Milk cases for storage bins

12"

Turpentine, Paint remover, solvent

40"

Bottom 3½ inches is toe space

1x4

1x12

STUDY AND BED LOFT

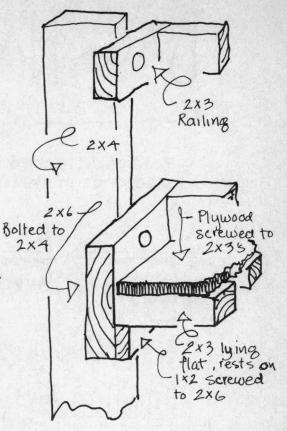

2x3 Railing

2x4

2x6 Bolted to 2x4

Plywood screwed to 2x3s

2x3 lying flat, rests on 1x2 screwed to 2x6

CONNECTION OF UPRIGHT 2x4 AND BED LOFT

Lofts are now common solutions to problems of too little space. There is a book, *The Loft Book*, that deals with this subject alone and shows in good detail how to plan and build one.

This loft is planned around a full size mattress (54 by 76 inches), desk space, and a couch. A nine foot ceiling is about the lowest that could contain such a structure, and still be used by adults. The five-foot headroom for the couch area is tight at that. The structure stands without connections to floor, ceiling, or walls. Its essence is a box of 2x6s framing the mattress, and eight 2x4 legs tied together with plywood gussets, making the structure rigid. Lag screws hold the 2x6 box together. The detail drawing shows how the box supports the 2x3 slats and the plywood. The 2x4 legs bolt to the 2x6s with 3/8- by 5-inch carriage bolts (the nuts are recessed so no one gets snagged). The gussets screw to the 2x4s and run in two directions. They also support the desk and the shelves above it, and form the back, sides, and bottom of the couch. The ladder is made of 2x4s and bolts to one of the leg pairs.

Skill Level: Basic, but lengthy in execution

Tools: Basic plus sabre saw or portable power saw

See also: Jim Wilson, *The Loft Book*. Philadelphia: Running Press, 1975.

Materials:
   3 sheets 3/4" x 4' x 8' plywood
   2 12-ft. 2x6s
   10 8-ft. 2x4s
   6 10-ft. 2x3s
   30 3/8" x 5" carriage bolts
   30 3/8" x 2-1/2" lag screws
   Box (100) 1-1/2" no. 8 screws

STUDY AND BED LOFT

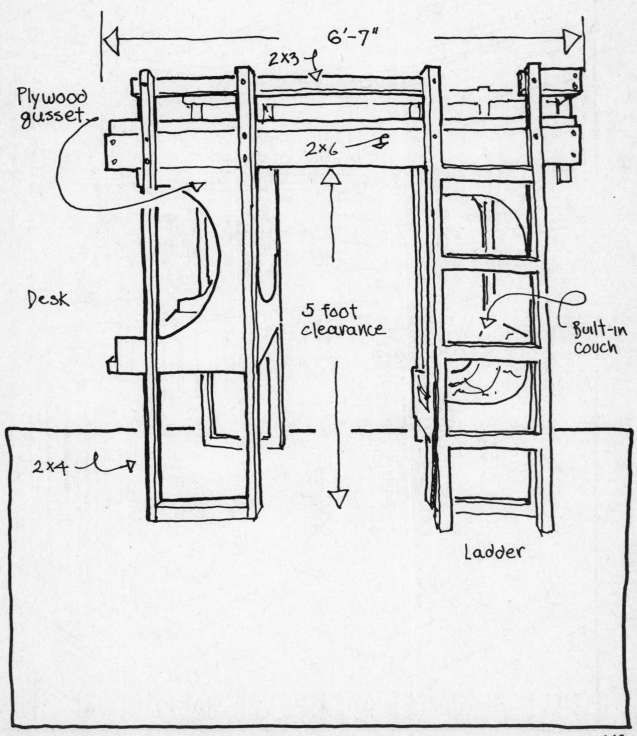

6'-7"

2X3

Plywood gusset

2×6

Desk

5 foot clearance

Built-in couch

2×4

Ladder

PORCH SITTING PLACE

Wind chime

2×4 supported
by blocks at ends

Clothes line

Cable reel
side

Solid
wooden box

TYPICAL WOODEN BACK PORCH IN BOSTON

PORCHES AND BALCONIES

I have seen old people sitting on their porches feeling the day, reading, watching, at home yet outside in their own place. I have seen parties on small porches, and parades in streets going by porches alive with smiling faces. I have seen laundry blowing colorfully in the breeze on porches. I have seen porches crammed with stuff stored there, and ones obviously unused at all. I have seen apartment towers stacked with blank unused balconies. I have loved porches and wondered why so many are neglected. Maybe it's fear of unsound old porches, or landlords who don't like kids playing there, or lack of privacy, or too much sun, or not enough, or maybe the porches are too small. There are probably other problems, too. Some problems have solutions, others do not, and some are not problems at all.

This chapter suggests a few ways to make porches more usable. No matter how small, a porch is useful. In Boston an east- or southeast-facing porch is great. It's a pleasant place to eat breakfast or drink coffee; it's shady in the afternoon, and the coolest place on a hot summer night. Southern- and western-facing porches are hotter, but lattices help provide cooling shade and extra privacy if you're too exposed. A north-facing porch gets sun only in summer mornings and evenings, which makes it great in the summer but not as nice in the spring and fall. Enclosing it with windows will help by cutting off breezes and holding some of the heat that comes from the house. I wonder how one of those new apartment towers would look if all the porches were either glassed-in (each one differently), or covered with lattices, or decked with plants hanging in baskets or climbing up wires. I think it would look like somebody lived there!

PORCH PLANTING RACK

A container garden is a reasonable alternative to a yard garden when no yard is available. I've grown delicious tomatoes on my porch, and books I've read say you can grow almost any vegetable successfully in containers: corn, cucumbers, beans, onions, tomatoes, lettuce. Any container that will hold a few gallons of soil will do. I've used wooden crates from fruit stands, home-made boxes, and five-gallon plastic buckets from the local bakery. You can simply arrange the buckets on the porch, but if it's a wooden porch, put a couple of bricks under each container so the floor won't rot. The problem is that the porch soon gets cluttered with containers and paraphernalia.

The planting rack shown is one solution to the clutter problem. You can use the rack inside during the winter as a potting area or plant stand, and as a place to start seedings in the spring. The extra-long legs allow the stand to be more flexible: clear plastic can be attached to them to enclose the tray and make it a cold frame; grow lights can be hooked to them also if used indoors.

The legs are 2x3s with holes carefully spaced and drilled for stove bolts that hold the trays. The trays are 1x4s screwed together with a 3/4-inch plywood bottom. The stove bolts make the rack's height adjustable, and permit it to be disassembled for moving or storage. You can treat the wood with wood preservative. It won't hurt the plants.

Skill Level: Basic (accurate measuring and drilling)

Tools: Basic Kit

Materials:
- 24 l.f. 1x4
- 3/4" x 24" x 60" exterior-grade plywood
- 24 l.f. 2x3
- 36 2" no. 8 wood screws or 1/2 lb. 8d finishing nails
- 16 2-1/2" x 1/4" stove bolts and nuts
- 32 washers for the bolts
- Wood preservative

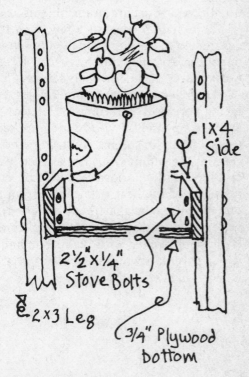

1x4 Side

2½" x ¼" Stove Bolts

2x3 Leg

3/4" Plywood bottom

CROSS SECTION

Porch Planting Rack

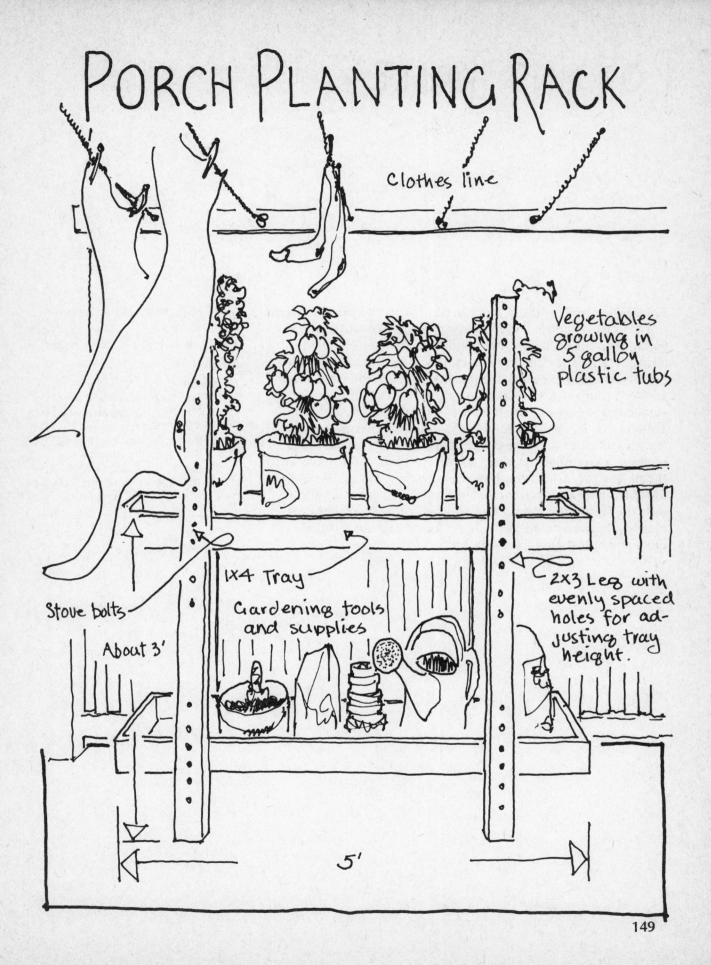

Clothes line

Vegetables growing in 5 gallon plastic tubs

Stove bolts

1x4 Tray
Gardening tools and supplies

About 3'

2x3 Leg with evenly spaced holes for adjusting tray height.

5'

POTTING TABLE

This table is built entirely of 1x2s. Similar to the workbench on p. 141, the top and the shelf below nail to three cleats, and the legs bolt to the cleats. Begin by building the legs. Include the cleats because they are also crosspieces in the legs. Clamp the two cleats and one crossbrace (as shown in the end-view sketch) between four verticals. Make sure all the parts are properly positioned so the legs will be straight and the table flat, and drill 1/4-inch holes for stove bolts in the indicated places. All three legs should be exactly the same. Label the parts for easy reassembly, and remove the cleats to nail the shelf and top pieces to them. Nail the strips with 6d finishing or box nails, leaving a 3/4-inch space between them. Use a board on edge as a spacer. Bolt the legs to the cleats. The drawings show two more crossbraces. These brace the table in the long direction. Fit these now, and bolt them to the cleats.

Skill Level: Basic; but accuracy is necessary

Tools: Basic and 4 3" "C" clamps

See also: Workbench, p. 140.

Materials:
- 12 6-ft. 1x2s for top and shelf
- 12 3-ft. 1x2s for leg verticals
- 6 15-in. 1x2s for cleats
- 3 3-ft. 1x2s for cross bracing
- 2 4-ft. 1x2s for cross bracing
- 22 2-1/2" x 1/4" stove bolts
- 1/2 lb. 6d finishing or box nails

POTTING TABLE

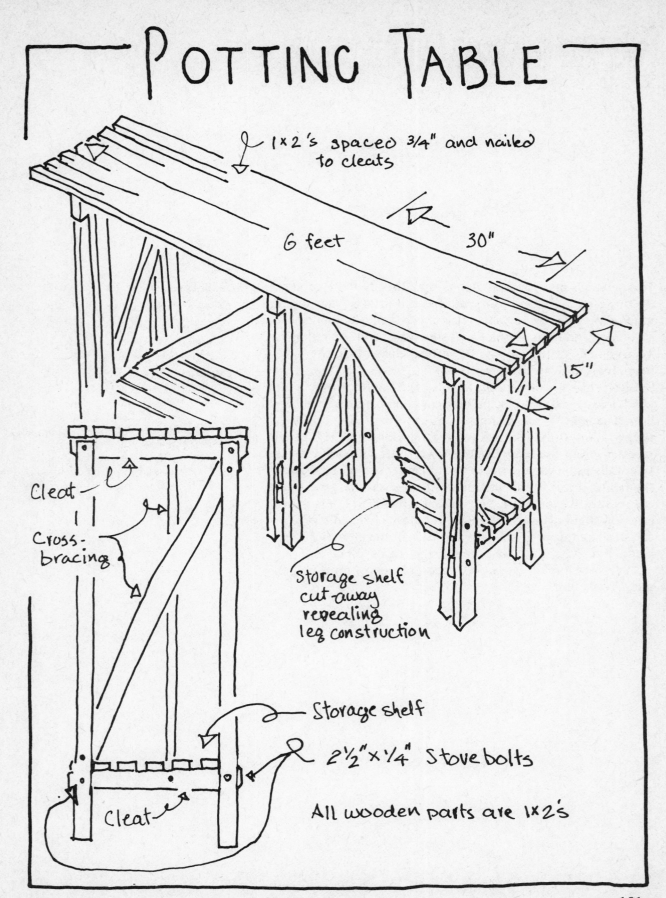

1 x 2's spaced 3/4" and nailed to cleats

6 feet

30"

15"

Cleat

Cross-bracing

storage shelf cut away revealing leg construction

Storage shelf

2½" x ¼" Stove bolts

Cleat

All wooden parts are 1x2's

Screen with Shelf

This screen is meant for a balcony that already has a good railing (in this case, wood and iron), but has too little privacy or too much sun to be comfortable. The screen stands behind the existing railing and bolts to the floor, side walls, and the railing itself. To complement the railing, the vertical elements in the screen line up with the verticals in the railing.

Bolt the sill to the floor. In this case, the floor is concrete. Use a masonry drill to drill a hole for an expansion shield and lag bolt. Toenail the four major verticals to the sill and bolt them to the railing with 3/8- by 5-inch carriage bolts. (The nuts will be recessed.) Nail the top piece to the verticals, and bolt it to the side walls using angle irons (or in a manner similar to that of the railing). Bolt the shelf supports to the verticals, and notch the 2x8 to fit around the verticals, and nail it to the supports. Position the short cross pieces with blocks clamped to the verticals at the appropriate height, and toenail the crosspieces in place. Finally, cut and nail the short verticals in place.

Salvaged lumber (redwood, cedar, or yellow pine are perfect) would work well for this project.

Skill Level: Basic

Tools: Basic and two 3-inch "C" clamps

See also: Entrance Trellis, p. 78.
Balcony Lattice, p. 154.
Glassed-in Balcony, p. 156.

Materials:
66 l.f. 2x4
18 l.f. 2x8
12 3/8" x 5" carriage bolts
5 lag bolts
5 lag shields
2 1-1/2 x 3/4" corner irons
1-1/2 lb. 8d galvanized common nails
1 lb. 10d galvanized common nails

SCREEN WITH SHELF

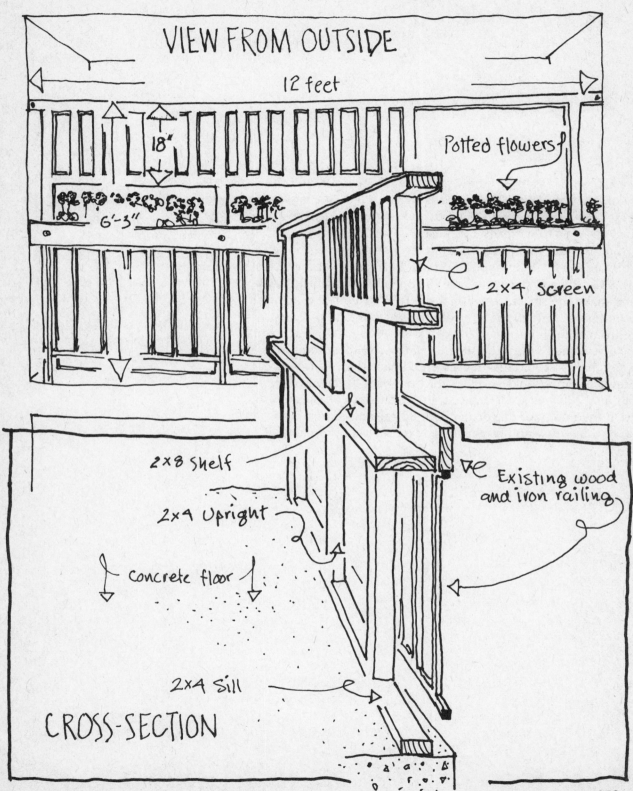

VIEW FROM OUTSIDE

12 feet

18"

6'-3"

Potted flowers

2×4 Screen

2×8 Shelf

2×4 Upright

concrete floor

Existing wood and iron railing

2×4 Sill

CROSS-SECTION

BALCONY LATTICE

There are two ideas in this drawing — the lattice itself, and the rods for hanging plants. The other day I saw a pile of coat-room wall racks in a salvage yard. They fit well with this idea, and only needed cleaning to be ready for reuse.

Build the lattice in sections and then bolt the units to the balcony railing or floor, and the ceiling. Salvaged 2x8s and 2x4s are fine for the structure. Measure the opening into which it will fit and make the structure 1/8-inch shorter. Drive 10d galvanized common nails through the sill from the bottom, and through the plate from the top into the vertical 2x4s — two nails in each end. Also toenail the 2x4s to the sill and plate with 8d galvanized common nails — four nails in each end. Space the verticals at whatever distance looks good to you: the ones in the drawing are about 12 inches apart. Space the 1x2 slats as you please also, either horizontally or diagonally. Use 8d galvanized common nails. Finish with wood preservative, exterior stain, or paint.

Skill Level: Basic

Tools: Basic

See also: Entrance Trellis, p. 78.
Screen with Shelf, p. 152.
Glassed-in Balcony, p. 156.

Materials:
2x4s for verticals and plate
2x8 for sill
1x2s for slats
Screws, nails, or bolts for mounting
10d and 8d galvanized common nails

BALCONY LATTICE

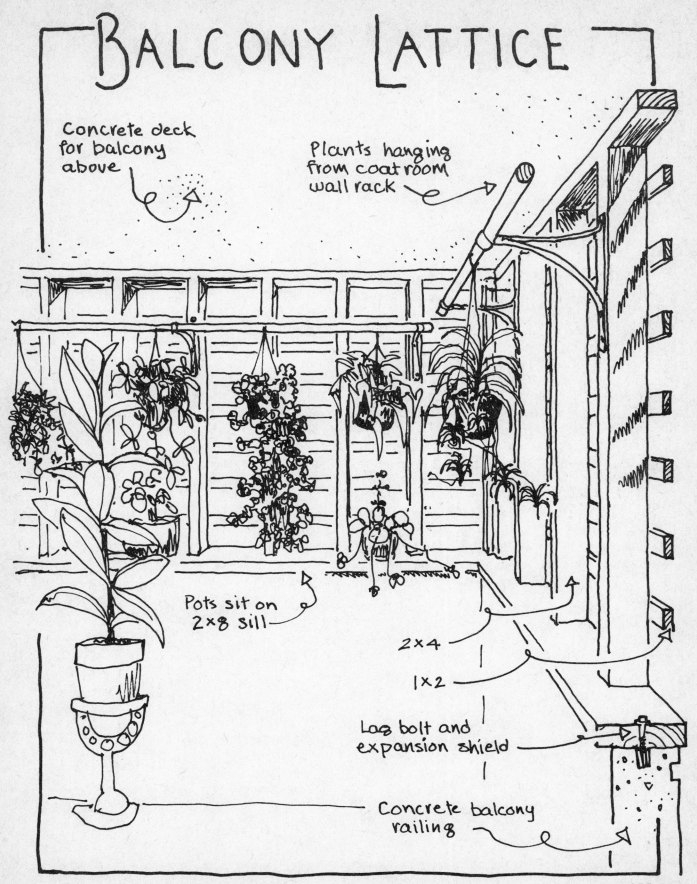

Concrete deck for balcony above

Plants hanging from coat room wall rack

Pots sit on 2×8 sill

2×4

1×2

Log bolt and expansion shield

Concrete balcony railing

GLASSED-IN BALCONY

The structure for these windows is the same as for the lattice on the previous page. But here the spacings of the vertical 2x4s depend upon the widths of whatever windows you get. Storm windows are common in salvage yards and currently cost about $6 a piece (in Boston) if the glass is intact. (This is about one-half the cost of the glass alone.) Probably it will be hard to find matching windows, so the design shows a way to use windows of different widths and lengths. Get enough windows to fill the given space. Build the structure to fit the windows. You must be sure the verticals *are vertical* and spaced 1/8- to 1/4-inch wider than the windows. One way to hold the windows in place is to nail 1x2 stops to the sides and tops of the openings and screw the windows to them. This will not be water-tight, but it will keep most of the water and wind away from the balcony. The use of screws will make it easier to remove windows for maintenance. Work carefully and neatly. You could paint the structure one color and the windows another. Instead of windows you could use screens, which also are available in salvage yards.

Skill Level: Basic

Tools: Basic

See also: Balcony Lattice, p. 154.
Balcony Screen, p. 152.
Entrance Trellis, p. 78.

Materials:
Collection of wooden storm windows
2x8 for sill
2x4s for verticals and plate
1x2s for stops
8d and 10d galvanized common nails for structure
6d galvanized finishing nails for stops
1-3/4" no. 8 wood screws for mounting windows

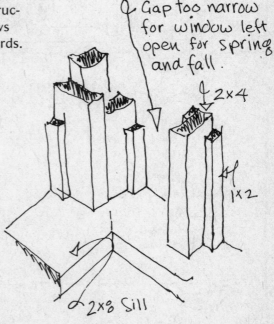

Gap too narrow for window left open for spring and fall.

2x4

1x2

2x8 Sill

Detail of Corner

156

GLASSED-IN BALCONY

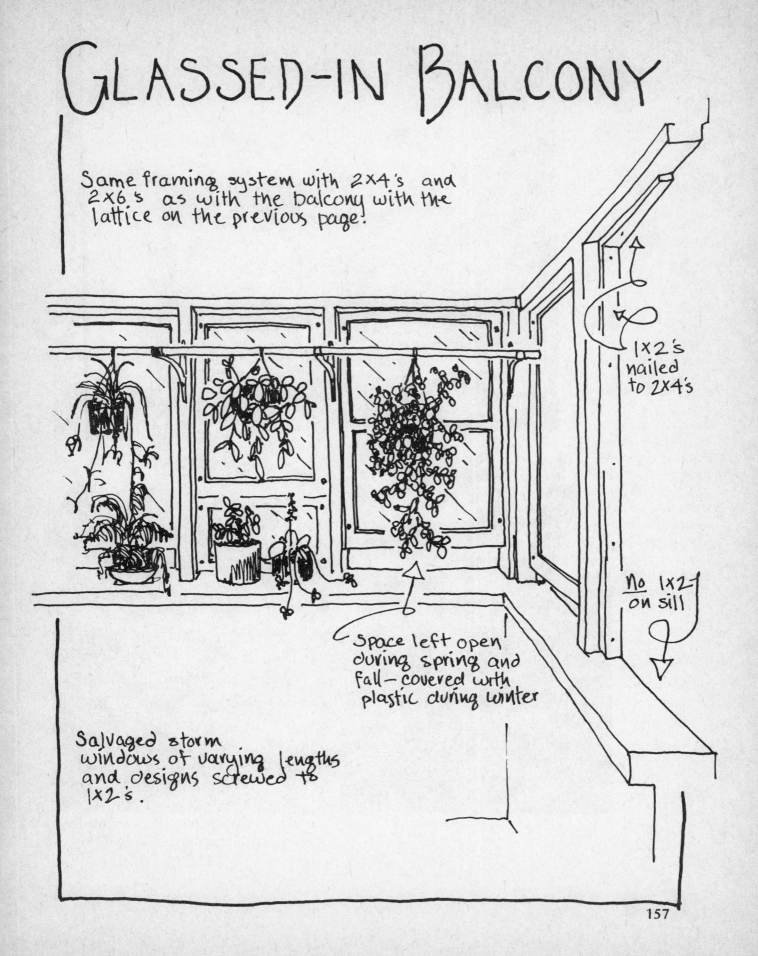

Same framing system with 2×4's and 2×6's as with the balcony with the lattice on the previous page.

1×2's nailed to 2×4's

No 1×2 on sill

Space left open during spring and fall — covered with plastic during winter

Salvaged storm windows of varying lengths and designs screwed to 1×2's.

Eating area with boxes used as a collage and shelves (p. 114)

Jan's museum-place medicine cabinet (pp. 100, 110)

Amanda's people behind an old frosted glass door

Kitchen cabinets made of old
drawers and wall panels cut for
doors. (pp. 128, 132)

Old drawers make up the top of this cabinet, and the cast iron grate redirects heat from existing in-floor vent. (pp. 128, 132)

Bakery boxes for dishes (p. 114)

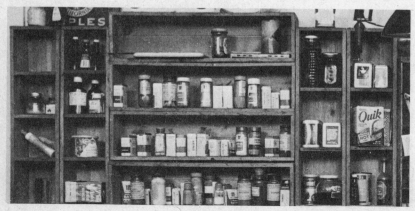

Shelves made from fish crates (p. 114)

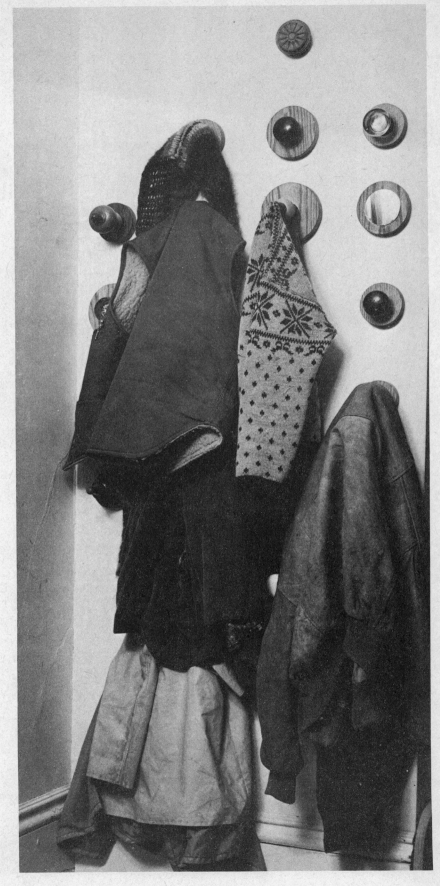

Doorknob coat hooks in the
front hall (p. 30)

Rebuilt stairway using
old oak lumber and
stair parts. (*See*
appendix)

Porch planting rack (p. 88)

Mailbox (p. 28)

Spice and canister shelves (p. 116)

Adjustable wall shelves for a workshop. (p. 14)

Jan's entry hall with
puzzle floor below.
(p. 74)

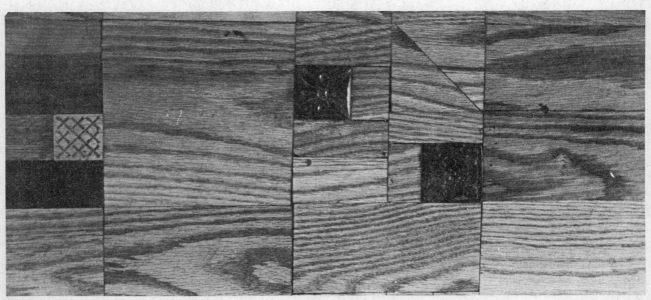

APPENDIX

Woodworking tools have remained basically the same for 2000 years. So the tools in your grandparents' garage or at a secondhand store are probably as good as new ones. But the old will require oiling to loosen joints and remove rust; they'll need sharpening and loving. This is especially worthwhile for tools that would be expensive if new, such as planes, hand drills, bit braces with bits, levels, and squares. A hammer with a broken handle is okay, as you can easily replace the handle.

Because it takes more effort to use a dull tool, you run the risk of losing control and hurting yourself if you neglect the situation. Many hardware stores sharpen tools at reasonable prices. This is an especially worthwhile investment for saw blades, which, if sharpened incorrectly, will not cut straight. You can use files and a sharpening stone to sharpen your own chisels, planes, and wood-boring bits. Sharpening is an art in itself but you can learn enough on your own to keep your tools sharp between professional sharpenings. (See the section on sharpening procedures, p. 178).

Power tools are time and muscle savers. Power saws will produce finer though not always more accurate cuts than handsaws. Because of their inherent danger, always read the instructions that come with them.

A zig-zag or folding rule is normally six feet long, divided into 1/16-inch intervals. Some have a sliding metal extension that makes it easier to take inside dimensions, such as the distance between window stops. They have a tendency to break at their folding joints, so compare models and buy one that has sturdy joints.

ZIG-ZAG RULE

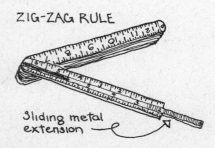

Sliding metal extension

Tape measures normally come in lengths of 6, 8, 10, 12, and 50 feet. I have always found the six- and eight-footers too short for general use. A tape is less cumbersome than a folding rule, but will not take inside dimensions quite as well. Tapes come in varying widths up to ¾ inch. You can buy replacement tapes. The hook at the end of the tape should slide (this allows you to take inside measurements), but it should also be sturdy. Check it.

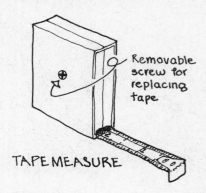

Removable screw for replacing tape

TAPE MEASURE

A framing square is the most versatile of measuring tools; I have seen thick volumes on its use alone. Most of the fancy shapes, cuts, and angles in houses were laid out with this tool — roof rafters, stairs, bay windows, cupolas. Beginners will find it invaluable just in keeping things square.

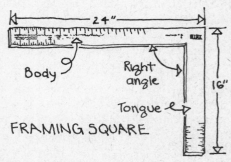

24"

Body

Right angle

16"

Tongue

FRAMING SQUARE

The try square and combination square are smaller, less versatile versions of the framing square. They are used for checking squareness of boards. I prefer the combination square because its sliding head can be used to copy dimensions accurately, and also because it can lay out a 45 degree angle, which is second in prevalence only to the 90 degree cut.

COMBINATION SQUARE

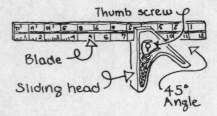

The level is used to check surfaces to see if they are level (horizontal) or plumb (vertical). They come in several sizes ranging from pocket-size, to the hand level (9 inches), and up. They are made of wood, aluminum, or magnesium. A metal level is more expensive, but it is more durable than wood, and the vials are replaceable. Another type of level is the line level, which is merely a fluid-filled vial that will hook over a string tied between two points. (The string is used as a reference line for laying out a fence, wall, or other structure not on a level surface.)

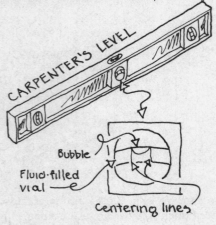

A chalk line is a tool for marking long straight lines on walls, floors, and ceilings. To use it, stretch the line taut across two marks (a V is a good mark because of the point). If you're alone, you can slip the clip over a nail and stretch the line taut against the floor with one hand; with the other, lift the line and let it snap back — thwack. It will leave a straight, precise, chalked line.

Hammers are available in a dozen or more types. They differ in their faces, claws, handles, size, and material. When buying a claw hammer, heft it to see if it feels good; check to see if the head is made of drop-forged steel (cast heads chip and the pieces fly); check to see if the claw will remove finishing nails (cheap hammers often will pull only a nail with a head on it). See section on nails, p.173. Two others you might need are a soft-face hammer, and a tack

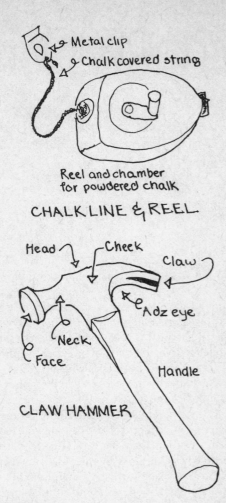

CHALK LINE & REEL

CLAW HAMMER

hammer. Use the soft-face hammer or a wooden mallet when working with a chisel.

Screwdrivers differ with respect to size and blade tip. Two major tip types correspond to two major screw slot types — Phillips, and straight-slot. See screws, page 173. The screwdriver should fit the screw you are using; the blade tip should fit snuggly into the screw slot, and be about the same width as the head of the screw. It should

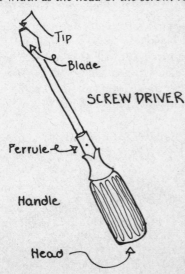

SCREW DRIVER

not be worn round (you can grind or file a rounded blade square). If you use the largest possible screwdriver, the job will be made easier. Screwdrivers come in short lengths for tight places, and also offset for working around corners.

Saws vary in general shape and form, as well as in the number, size, shape, and direction of their teeth. The number and size of teeth determine the fineness of the cut. The more and smaller the teeth, the finer the cut. Saws are sold according to the number of points or teeth per inch of blade. Saws for cutting wood fall into two major categories — ripsaws and crosscut saws. A ripsaw will cut properly only along the grain of the wood — this is usually the long direction through the board. It does this task quickly and with surprising ease in control. (You can correct a cut that is going crooked by twisting the handle and taking short, gentle strokes.) A crosscut saw will cut both across and along the grain, but it does the latter with much less speed than the ripsaw. It is difficult to tell the difference between the two types of saws at a first glance. The differences are found in the size and shape of their teeth. A ripsaw has 5½ or 6 points per inch and the teeth are similar to chisels in shape. Crosscut saws have 7 to 11 points per inch, and the teeth are similar to knives. Since lumber comes in varying widths (see Lumber, p. 172), the ripsaw is used less frequently than the crosscut saw. I would recommend a 20-inch 10-point crosscut saw as the first one to buy for household use. A 10-point crosscut saw will give smooth cuts appropriate to most of the projects in this book. Unless you'll only use it a few times, buy a good saw. A cheap saw dulls quickly, and then will cut slowly and worse, crookedly.

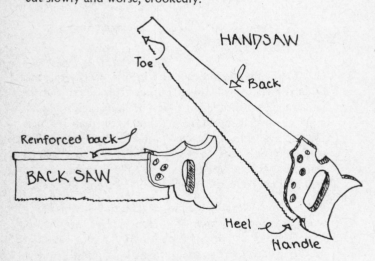

HANDSAW

Toe

Back

Reinforced back

BACK SAW

Heel

Handle

A backsaw is another useful saw to have. It is a fine-toothed crosscut saw with a reinforced back. It is used to make short, precise cuts, as in miter cuts on picture frames and moldings. It is often used with a miter box. This will guide the saw at a particular angle while cutting.

The compass saw is made to fit into tight places. You can also use it to cut holes and slots. To start a hole-type cut,

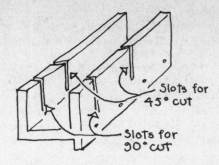

Slots for 45° cut

Slots for 90° cut

SIMPLE WOODEN MITER BOX

drill a hole larger than the tip of the saw blade. Then begin from that point with the compass saw.

The hacksaw is a fine-toothed saw for cutting metal. It is good at home for shortening bolts and cutting rods, tubing, pipe, and nails.

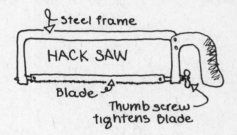

Steel frame

HACK SAW

Blade

Thumb screw tightens blade

Planes were once indispensable to all woodworking. Today most wood comes milled (preplaned) to exact dimensions, smoothed, and squared. This eliminates the most difficult planing operations. Since it is possible to work without a plane, you may choose to do so. But if you persevere and practice, you will probably want the quality of your work to improve. Most people use planes today for smoothing rough edges, trimming boards (especially doors) that are only slightly too large, and rounding or beveling sharp corners. Two planes will suffice for these operations: the block plane and the smoothing plane. The block plane, about five inches long, is made for smoothing end grain. Wood planed on its end grain tends to split at the edges. One way to avoid this is to plane from the two edges, working toward the center of the board. Because it is short, the block plane does not work well for smoothing long board edges. The smoothing plane, about eight inches long, is better suited to this task. A proper lesson on using and caring for planes would take more space than we have available here. For now, observe your plane and experi-

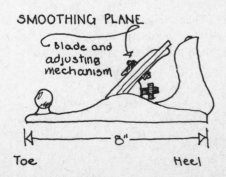

SMOOTHING PLANE

blade and adjusting mechanism

8"

Toe   Heel

ment with it. Notice what the adjustments do, and keep the blade sharp. See Sharpening Procedures, p. 178.

A chisel is the tool to use for cutting insets, such as gains for hinges (see Hanging Doors, p. 176). Chisels come in sizes from 1/8 inch to 2 inches across the blade. A 1/2- or 3/4-inch chisel will suffice for most applications in this book. A chisel is dangerous when sharp and *more* dangerous when dull. A dull chisel is dangerous because you have to use more force, and so are more likely to lose control. If you buy a chisel, also buy a sharpening stone. (Note that you should sharpen the chisel each time you use it — see Sharpening Procedure, p. 178.) I have cut myself more than once using chisels improperly. Clamp your work so that both hands are free to control the chisel. I push the handle with one hand and control the blade with the other. *Don't* hit a chisel with a steel headed hammer. Use your palm or a soft-faced hammer or mallet.

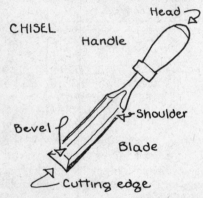

CHISEL

Head

Handle

Bevel

Shoulder

Blade

Cutting edge

Surform tools are relatively new variants of the plane and file families. They come in many sizes and shapes, but they all have the same cheese-grater-like blade design. It is a good substitute for a plane, but when it gets dull you must replace the blade. I recommend the *pocket size* Surform as the most useful here.

POCKET SIZE SURFORM

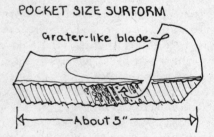

Grater-like blade

About 5"

All power tools come with good instructions for their use and care. The following information is intended only as background for a few power tools to consider collecting. I would suggest buying as need for them arises.

Portable electric drills are probably the most popular of electric tools. They are easy and safe to use, inexpensive to buy, and versatile. Besides drilling holes, they will buff, sand, grind, polish, and drive screws. I would recommend getting one with a 3/8-inch chuck, and variable speed motor.

PORTABLE ELECTRIC DRILL

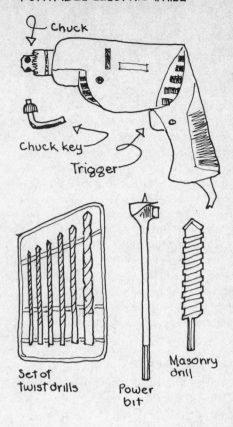

Chuck

Chuck key

Trigger

Set of twist drills

Power bit

Masonry drill

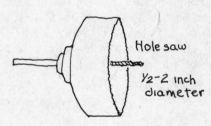

Hole saw

1/2-2 inch diameter

Drill bits come individually and in sets. Twist-drill sets usually range from 1/16 to 1/4 inch in diameter, with sizes increasing by either 1/32 or 1/64 of an inch. Sets containing drills smaller than 1/16 inch and larger than 1/4 inch are also available. Twist drills will cut metal as well as wood. Power bits come in sizes from 1/4 up to 1 inch in diameter and cut wood only. Use only masonry bits to drill into concrete, block, brick, and mortar.

A portable power saw is a muscle- and time-saving tool. When used properly and with practice, it will produce a finer cut than a hand saw. You can buy or make guides to use along with this saw to improve its accuracy. The saw comes in sizes according to blade diameter. A good size for home use is a 7- or 7-1/4-inch. They also vary according to motor horsepower. The greater the horsepower, the easier the cut, and the longer the life of the saw. There are blades for every sort of job: ripping, crosscut, combination, plywood, miter, metal, masonry. The combination blade is best for general use. If you are using plywood and you need a clean cut, get a plywood blade, but don't use this blade to cut anything else. The miter or planer blade will give a fine cut in ordinary woods. It takes practice to use this tool well, but learning is easy. The best way is to ask an experienced friend to work with you the first time you use one.

PORTABLE POWER SAW

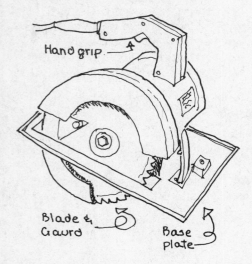

A *sabre saw* is a portable jigsaw that can make straight and curved cuts. It is easier and safer to use than the power saw, but not as powerful. Like the power saw, it uses a variety of blades for different materials and cuts.

SABRE SAW

Portable power sanders are of two basic types. One is orbital, or dual action, a so-called vibrating sander. A rectangular platform holds a piece of sandpaper, and moves rapidly back and forth or in small circles. It takes the drudgery out of putting a smooth finish on a piece of woodwork. The other type is a belt sander, with an endless, tractorlike belt of sandpaper moving at high RPM. This is a great tool, especially if you use a lot of old wood. It will quickly remove an old finish, dirt, and grit from a board. Its tractorlike configuration prevents it from getting into corners, so its use should be limited to flat surfaces without inside corners.

DUAL ACTION SANDER

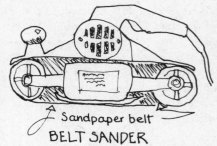

BELT SANDER

TOOL KITS

First Kit: hammer
screwdriver
tape measure or folding rule
common sense

Basic Kit: all the above plus:
crosscut saw
try square
hand or electric drill
level
framing square
pliers
adjustable wrench (crescent wrench)
more screwdrivers:
    2 Phillips
    3 straight-slot
jackknife
Surform tool

Cabinetry: all the above plus:
combination square
backsaw
miter box
ripsaw
minimum of two 3-inch "C" clamps
2 sawhorses
block plane
chalk line
chisel
sharpening stone
mallet or soft-faced hammer
a work bench with a vise is useful but not
    absolutely necessary

Lumber

Wood is made of fibers, called the *grain*, that run vertically. The rings in the end of a board display yearly growth across the grain. Because grain is directional, the strength of wood is directional. It is strong along the grain, and weak across the grain. Consider this when working with wood.

Lumber is defined in two broad categories, hardwoods and softwoods. Hardwoods come from deciduous trees, such as oak, maple, mahogany, birch, walnut, cherry, ash, etc. Softwoods are from coniferous trees like pine, spruce, hemlock, cedar, redwood, etc. Though not strictly true, the hardwoods are harder and qualitatively prettier than the softwoods, and so produce better furniture and cabinetry. They are also more difficult to work. Softwoods are used exclusively in wood construction, and lumber yards sell much more softwood than hardwood.

Lumber is also categorized into grades, but it is probably simpler to tell the salesperson how you plan to use the wood. (S)he may suggest a few options. Look at and compare what is available. For most projects in this book requiring boards, "no. 2 common pine" (boards with knotholes in them) will do. However, don't buy it if it is warped.

Lumber is sold by the board foot (board measure), or by the lineal foot (linear, or running foot). *By the lineal foot* simply means according to the length of the piece. *Board measure* means according to the number of square feet contained in a piece. A board said to be one inch thick and twelve inches wide contains one board foot for each lineal foot. Likewise, a board two inches thick and six inches wide also contains one board foot per lineal foot.

Dimensions of wood are based on size before curing and milling. Lumber from the forest is first cut to rough sizes. Then it is cured or dried. Lumber is either dried in a kiln or in the open air. Once dried, the lumber is milled. In this process the faces and edges are smoothed and squared. Wood called one inch thick is actually one three-quarters of an inch thick. Dimensions from two to six inches are actually one-half inch less. A one by two (1 x 2) is 3/4 inch by 1-1/2 inches. Dimensions from eight inches are three-quarters of an inch less. A 1 x 8 is 3/4 inch by 7-1/4 inches.

Plywood

Plywood is made of thin layers (plys, or veneers) of wood glued (laminated) in a sandwich fashion, with the grain of each layer turned 90 degrees to adjacent layers. The result is a large panel that is strong in all directions. Most plywood comes in 4- by 8-foot sheets with thicknesses from 3/16 inch to 1-3/16 inches. The two outside layers are called face and back. Each sheet of plywood is stamped with the grades of the face and back. The grades are the letters: N (natural finish, free of open defects), A (smooth and paintable), B (solid surface with holes patched), C

(knotholes present), and D (large knotholes). Plywood is also labeled marine, exterior, or interior; marine plywood is the most resistive to water. If you're not sure what grade of plywood to buy, tell the salesperson how you will use it.

The finest plywoods available are the solid birch, often called Finnish or Baltic. Not all yards sell it. It has more plys than standard plywood and all the plys are of top-grade veneers. The edges are clean and beautiful when sanded and finished. It is a great material for cabinetry and furniture. Baltic plywood is normally sold in sheets that are 5 feet square, or 4 feet by 6 feet. Because of its cost, however, it is also sold by the square foot.

Homasote

Homasote is a soft, pressed, cardboard-like substance. Like plywood, it is sold in 4- by 8-foot sheets. It is 1/2-inch thick. Though not pretty, it is an excellent tackboard surface. Its appearance is greatly improved with a coat of latex wall paint, or a covering of fabric like muslin or canvas.

Masonite and Particle Board

These are two products made by pressing wood fibers into sheets. Masonite, or hardboard, is hard and brittle, with smaller fibers than particle board. Masonite is thin (1/8- to 1/4-inch). Both products come in 4- by 8-foot sheets. They say you can use either of these materials as subfloors and backing for tiles, but I wouldn't recommend it. I prefer to use masonite as a backing for shelves and cabinets (1/8 inch thick), and particle board for cheap shelving (at least 3/4 inch thick).

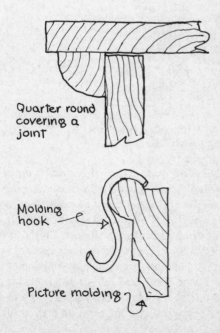

Quarter round covering a joint

Molding hook

Picture molding

Moldings

Often hardware stores, as well as lumber yards, sell a variety of moldings. Two useful types are sketched here. The quarter-rounds and other similar moldings can effectively cover and/or strengthen a joint where two boards join. Picture molding is specially shaped so that when it is nailed to the wall, pictures can be hung from it without the worry of any visible nail-hole damage once the picture is removed.

Nails

Besides the nails sketched here, there are many other special-purpose nails — concrete, masonry, flooring, roofing, shingle, fiberboard, and so on.

Sizes range from 2d to 60d. The "d" is read as "penny," and originally referred to the cost of 100 nails of the given size. A 60d nail is about six inches long and a 2d about one inch. Normal sizes to use are 4d through 10d.

Brads are small finishing nails and are sold according to gauge and length. (Gauge refers to diameter.)

A good rule of thumb for nailing is to use nails that are three times as long as the board being nailed is thick. If the wood splits when nailed, try dulling the nail tip by hitting it with a hammer. If that fails, predrill a hole slightly smaller than the nail.

NAILS

Common nail: for general construction

Annular ring nail: for wall board, & under layment

Finishing nail: for finish work

Wood Screws

Wood screws differ in length, thickness, head configuration, and material. The sketches show different heads and slots. Lengths range from 1/4 to 6 inches. Thicknesses range according to an arbitrary set of sizes from 1 to 18. Number 1 is the smallest size. Numbers 6, 8, and 10 are the most generally used sizes. Most screws are either steel or brass. Brass screws, softer than steel, are more difficult to use, and also more expensive, but they don't rust. I usually use steel screws except for special situations where I need a more decorative appearance.

It's easier to drive a screw if you predrill a hole for it. The hole's diameter should be slightly smaller than that of the screw. There is an attachment for electric drills, often called a screwmate drill, that is specially made for screw holes. It comes in sizes that correspond to screw sizes.

SCREWS

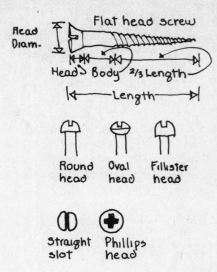

Round head   Oval head   Fillister head

Straight slot   Phillips head

SCREWMATE DRILL

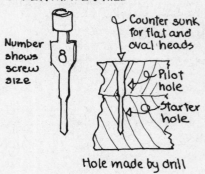

Number shows screw size

Counter sunk for flat and oval heads

Pilot hole

Starter hole

Hole made by drill

OTHER SCREW DEVICES

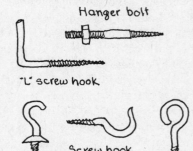

Hanger bolt

"L" screw hook

Screw hook

Cup hook   Screw eye

Countersink a flathead screw. Don't countersink a round-head screw, but put a washer between its head and the wood to distribute the pressure between them.

You can use a drill to drive the screw into its hole. There are screwdriver bits to fit various screw sizes, but you can cut the blade off of an old screwdriver and use it instead.

Bolts

The sketches show some types of bolts. Bolts are useful for connecting structural members and/or for joining pieces which you may want to dismantle and reassemble repeatedly. Stove bolts are for lighter pieces, such as one-inch boards (see The Storage Wall, p. 12). Carriage bolts, machine bolts, and lag bolts (also called lag screws) are for two-bys (2 x 4s, 2 x 6s, etc.) and larger pieces. A carriage bolt has below the head a square shoulder that keeps the bolt from turning when you tighten the nut. As you do with screws, put washers between most bolt heads and wood, and also between nut and wood. (No washer is needed between head of *carriage* bolt and wood.) In other words, if a washer will fit, use it.

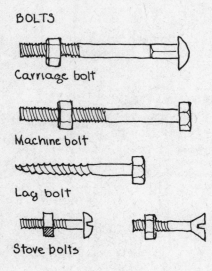

BOLTS

Carriage bolt

Machine bolt

Lag bolt

Stove bolts

Molly Bolts

Molly bolts are for fastening things heavier than a few pounds to hollow walls, when you can't nail or screw into wall studs (see drawings at beginning of wall section, p. 2). To install a Molly bolt: (1) Drill a hole of the size specified on the package; (2) insert the shield and bolt; (3) tighten the bolt until it is stiff. Now you can remove and reinsert the bolt as necessary; the shield is permanently anchored. A single Molly bolt will hold as much weight as 200 pounds on a wall (considerably less from the ceiling). They come in sizes from "XS" to "XL" (3/4-inch to 3-1/2-inches). An "S" is about right for normal use.

Expansion Shields

Expansion shields are used to fasten things to solid plaster, masonry, and concrete *walls* or *floors* (they pull out). They come in different sizes from small enough to use with standard wood screws to much larger, to use with expansion bolts. Use common sense to decide what's big enough. (It's best to opt for slightly large if you're not sure.)

HOW MOLLY BOLTS WORK

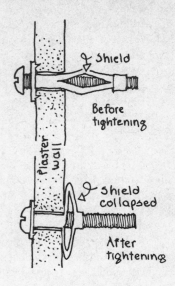

Shield

Before tightening

Shield collapsed

After tightening

Plaster wall

EXPANSION SHIELD

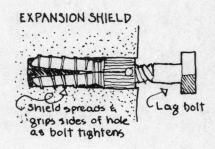

Shield spreads & grips sides of hole as bolt tightens

Lag bolt

Drill the specified hole to the specified depth, and insert the shield and loose bolt or screw. Tightening the bolt forces the shield to spread and grip the sides of the hole.

Hinges

Hinges come in a great variety of sizes and configurations for their different uses. I try to use brass or brass-plated hinges whenever possible. They look better and last longer than steel. One hinge is made of two leaves. The selling dimenions are as in the drawing. They usually come with appropriate screws. If not, buy hinges and screws of the same metal, because different metals corrode each other

A HINGE

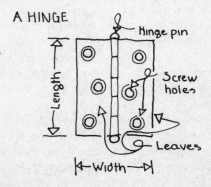

Hinge pin

Screw holes

Length

Leaves

Width

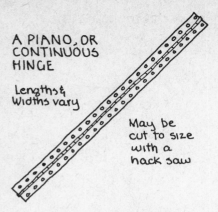

A PIANO, OR CONTINUOUS HINGE

Lengths & Widths vary

May be cut to size with a hack saw

when they come in contact. Hinges come in pairs (two hinges or four leaves). To install hinges, see Hanging Doors p. 176.

Braces and Plates

Hardware stores have hardware for every task. These are a few types that are useful when building new or reinforcing old boxes and frames.

BRACES AND PLATES

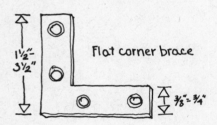

Flat corner brace

1½"–3½"

⅜"–¾"

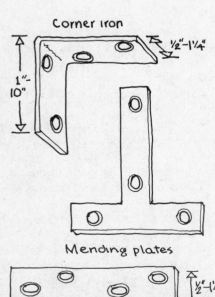

Corner iron

½"–1¼"

1"–10"

Mending plates

½"–1⅛"

2"–12"

Joining Wood

Butt Joint:
Requires square ends making flush joint held in place by nails or screws.

Reinforced Butt Joint:
The corner block allows the butt joint itself to be sloppier.

Mitered Joint:
For moldings and trims applied around doors, windows, and other openings.

Lap Joints and Notches:
Made by two to four parallel saw cuts cleaned out with a chisel. A neat type of joint, also resists twisting.

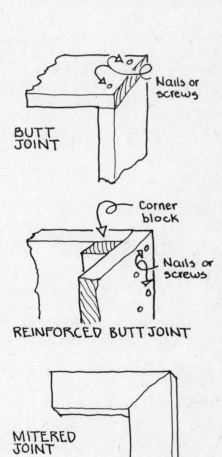

Nails or screws

BUTT JOINT

Corner block

Nails or screws

REINFORCED BUTT JOINT

MITERED JOINT

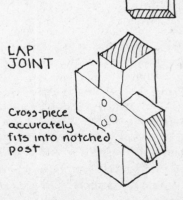

LAP JOINT

Cross-piece accurately fits into notched post

Hanging Doors

This is a task which requires great accuracy and care. It is the most difficult you'll encounter in this book. But if you're going to get beyond bare basics, understanding hinges is an important skill to learn. Before doing your own hinges, look at the ways in which various doors hang — doors to rooms, cabinets, trunks, chests, boxes. Notice where hinges are located; examine kinds of hinges and their sizes relative to door or lid dimensions; observe how they connect to the door and frame, how the door looks (particularly at the edges), how the frame and jamb look (the jamb is the surface within door frames to which the hinges connect); notice the amount of clearance between doors and jambs.

Notice also the differences between standard cabinet doors and room doors. (That cabinet doors usually have a rabet — a notch — along the backs of the four edges of the door that allows the door to cover the space between door and frame.) With the tools suggested for projects in this book, the rabet is difficult — though not impossible — to produce. The following instructions are for one alternative method of hanging cabinet doors.

Steps:

1. Make the frame.
2. Trim the door.
3. Mark hinge locations and cut gains.
4. Set the hinges.
5. Make adjustments.

Step One: a Frame

This simple frame is four 1 x 2 strips nailed and glued to a box or cabinet made of 3/4-inch boards or plywood. The notched cut at the ends of the top and bottom strips simplifies the problem of preventing the 1 x 2s from twisting off the cabinet. To ensure that the door will fit the opening, make sure that the frame is square, and that none of the strips bow in or out.

Step Two: Cutting or Trimming the Door

If you designed the cabinet around doors you already have, as in the greenhouse, and the bath storage cabinet, trimming should be unnecessary or, at most, only a matter of a little planing. Fit doors to be 1/8 inch shorter and narrower than their openings. If you are using panel sections or homemade doors, you may need to cut the edges. Mark the cut lines, making sure they are square. You can use a scrap board clamped to the door as a cutting guide for a hand saw, sabre saw, or portable power saw. Cut the door a little large so that when you smooth the edges it will fit properly.

Step Three: Marking Hinge Locations and Cutting Gains

Locate hinges equal distances from top and bottom of doors — one or two hinge-lengths is about right. Set the

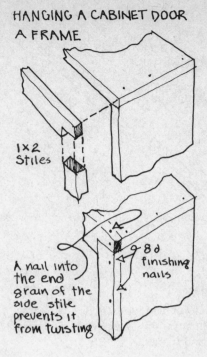

HANGING A CABINET DOOR
A FRAME

1 x 2 Stiles

A nail into the end grain of the side stile prevents it from twisting

9·8d finishing nails

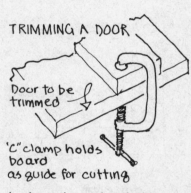

TRIMMING A DOOR

Door to be trimmed

'c' clamp holds board as guide for cutting

hinge on the door edge so that the hinge protrudes at least as far as the center of the hinge pin (otherwise the door will not open a full 180°). Mark around the hinge with a *sharp* pencil, making sure that the hinge is sitting squarely on the door's edge as you do so. I actually prefer to use the hinge to mark the length of the gain, and to use a combination square with its head slipped to the appropriate dimension to mark widths and depths of gain. If precise, these marks will make the following steps easier, and the door will hang well. The depth of the cut should be such that 1/32 to 1/16 inch will remain between door and frame after hanging.

Now there are four pencil lines on the door marking length, width, and depth of cut for gain.

Cut the gain with a chisel. A razor-sharp chisel makes the job easiest. Note when the gain is cut, the hinge should fit *exactly* (it shouldn't be able to slip up or down). So cut the gain at the inside edge of your pencil lines first, and then trim off more if necessary. To use the chisel, first rough in the cut with a series of parallel cuts, using a

MARKING LINES FOR THE GAIN

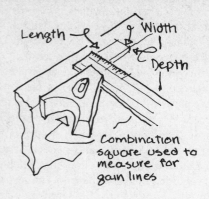

Length — Width

Depth

Combination square used to measure for gain lines

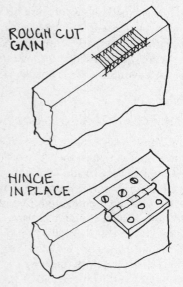

ROUGH CUT GAIN

HINGE IN PLACE

mallet to tap the chisel. Then, with *a hand on the handle* and *a hand on the blade*, pare the remaining material from the cut. Once the gains have been cut in the door, set the door in place and transfer the hinge locations to the frame. Repeat the cuts for gains there. It is possible to cut gains only in the door, or frame, but the extra cutting makes it easier to position hinges correctly when you hang the door.

Step Four: Setting the Hinges

Set a hinge in its gain. Use a nail or an awl to make points for screw pilot holes. Make this mark so that the hinge will be pulled more snugly into the gain as the screws tighten. Drill pilot holes for the screws slightly smaller than the screw diameter. This is especially necessary if you use brass screws and hinges (which I recommend), because brass is so soft that the head will twist off if the screw meets too much resistance. If screws don't go in easily, back them out and either redrill the pilot hole a little larger or wax the screw threads with paraffin or paste wax. I prefer to attach the hinges first to the door and then to the frame.

Step Five: Adjustments

If the door works to your satisfaction, congratulations. If it doesn't, it may be a good idea to let it be for now and make adjustments another day — this whole process of hanging doors can be a little frustrating, so don't let it get you down. (You may never really get your first door to hang exactly right anyway.)

If the door doesn't stay shut, or resists shutting, and it isn't rubbing anywhere, your gains are probably a little too deep. This hinge binding is remedied with a small piece of paper slipped between the hinge and the wood. Just loosen the screws and slip it in. The adjustments are a matter of common sense and patience, plus the willingness to tinker if you can't quite imagine what's wrong.

General Preparation for Floor Tiling

A standard floor with floor boards is *not* a suitable base for any tile. Small local bumps and hollows will cause hard tiles to wobble and come loose. The finest cracks between floor boards *will* show through any kind of flexible tile, eventually. The solution is a layer of plywood. A 3/8-inch thickness will suffice, if the floor is even to the eye. Otherwise, use 3/4-inch. Use exterior A–C grade, except in kitchens and baths. Marine plywood is required there because of water problems. Some people will tell you to use tempered masonite or hardboard (same thing). This is as good as marine plywood at resisting water, but it is difficult to pound the nails to hold it down flush with the surface. (Nailheads not flush will cause tiles to wobble.) Other people will suggest particle board. Don't use it. It won't hold up to water.

Drive annular ring nails (also called underlayment nails) into the plywood at 8-inch intervals. Their length should be at least three times as thick as the plywood. Allow a 1/32-inch gap between sheets for expansion, and offset the joints.

With a few exceptions, these same preparation rules apply for tiles on walls. Here, 1/4-inch plywood will be thick enough. Try to drive the nails so that they land in studs. Using a caulking gun, apply wallboard adhesive to the back of the plywood before nailing it up.

Once the surface is prepared, sweep the floor to remove dust (it will prevent floor adhesives from adhering). Two notions to be aware of when laying out the lines for starting tiles are: (1) walls are rarely parallel or perpendicular to each other, and (2) the tiles will probably not fit the room exactly and some will need to be cut. Generally, the grid of lines between tiles should be perpendicular and parallel to the wall where you enter the room. Cutting tiles isn't a difficult problem, but you don't want to have to lay tiles that are smaller than one-third of a full tile (small pieces don't adhere well, and they look bad). You can determine the remnant size mathematically or by actually laying tiles out on the floor. If the remnant is too

PREPARATION FOR FLOOR TILES

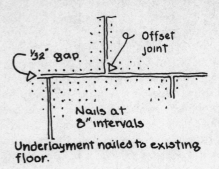

½″ gap — Offset joint

Nails at 8″ intervals

Underlayment nailed to existing floor.

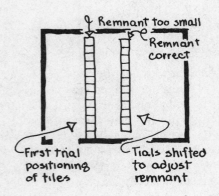

Remnant too small

Remnant correct

First trial positioning of tiles

Tiles shifted to adjust remnant

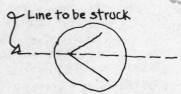

Line to be struck

A "V" inside a circle, the recommended mark for striking a line

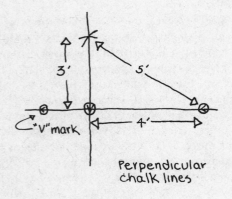

3′   5′

4′

"V" mark

Perpendicular chalk lines

small, you can remove one tile and shift all the tiles over half a tile, plus half the remnant.

Put a "V" mark at the edge of either a center tile or one on the far side. Now repeat entire process, going the other way across the room. The second "V" mark should be near the first one.

If you get the first tiles set correctly, the rest will follow easily. Precise cross lines which ensure that the first tiles are set at the correct place will be helpful. The best base line is a chalk line (see p. 168). Strike the first line parallel with the correct wall and through the first "V" mark. The second line is perpendicular to the first and through the second "V" mark. You can use some simple geometry to get the lines perpendicular. Recall that a triangle whose sides are three, four, and five units long is a right triangle. The only tools you'll need for this are a tape measure or a folding rule and a pencil. If the second "V" mark also falls on the first line, that will help. Measure three feet along the base line from the second "V". Measure four feet up from the "V" *roughly* perpendicular to the base and make a mark. Now measure five feet from the opposite end of the three-foot line segment, toward your four-foot mark. Adjust marks until dimensions are correct and marks cross. Strike a line through the "V" and the crossing marks. Layout is now complete.

Running New Light Fixtures Off Existing Outlet

These directions apply specifically to the medicine chest on p. 110. If there is an outlet on the wall where the cabinet is to go, it should be easy to add wiring for the light fixtures at the top of the chest. If the new outlet is directly in front of the old, you can use the old outlet box. Just disconnect it from the wall and pull it forward into the new position (the old cable in the wall will probably be long enough to permit this). Turn off the electricity supplying that outlet; check it before touching the wires. Disconnect the existing outlet. Run one end of the new plastic cable (type NM 14 gauge 2 wire plus ground is one kind) into the back of the box. Connect the wires to a combination switch and outlet as shown — black wires to brass screws, white to silver-colored screws. Join the wires together with plastic "wire nuts." Connect the light fixtures to the cable as shown. Electrical work you do on your home should meet code requirements. If you are doing something different from what is shown here, or if your house is old and many things already run off one fuse, do a little further reading on this matter. (Sears sells a good pamphlet, *Simplified Electrical Repairs*, that explains things quite understandably.)

Don't let electricity frighten you — but do be careful.

Honing Chisels and Planes

Unless you can get a grinding wheel or are willing to use a file, you should have your chisels and plane blades professionally sharpened about as frequently as your saws (if you're careful with them in the meantime). Between grindings, you can hone chisel and plane blades to keep them in condition. You should hone a chisel nearly every time you use it. This will make the honing job easier and only a

RUNNING NEW LIGHT FIXTURES OFF EXISTING OUTLET USING COMBINATION SWITCH AND OUTLET

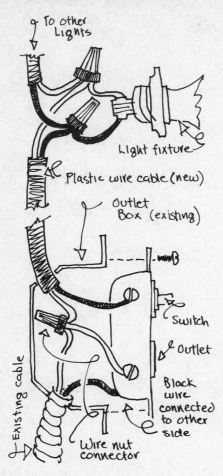

To other Lights

Light fixture

Plastic wire cable (new)

Outlet Box (existing)

Switch

Outlet

Black wire connected to other side

Wire nut connector

Existing cable

HONING A CHISEL OR PLANE

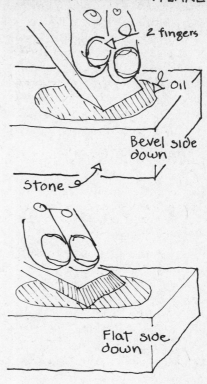

2 fingers

oil

Bevel side down

Stone

Flat side down

matter of quick routine (like brushing your teeth before seeing the dentist).

All you need is a sharpening stone of the same type used for knives, and some oil. To sharpen a chisel: (1) Put a few drops of oil on the stone; this will cause metal particles to float on rather than clog the stone. (2) Start sharpening the beveled edge — hold it flat against the stone with a finger. With the other hand grasp the handle in such a way that your wrist is comfortable. Move in small circles for a finer edge or back and forth for quicker cutting. (3) Check the blade frequently to be sure it is flat against the stone. Sharpening one side will cause a burr to form on the other. Continue alternately honing one side, then the other, until the burr comes off. The blade is then sharp. This process may be awkward at first, particularly the coordination between keeping the bevel flat and moving the blade.

Finishing Methods

Finishing is an art, and fine finishes require much time, patience, and skill. This section outlines a few simple methods.

Preparation

If appearance is a consideration, surface preparation should precede the actual finishing. Fill holes with wood dough or a mixture of glue and sawdust. Sand all the surfaces until roughness and stains are gone, paying close attention to joints and end grain. You can wrap sandpaper around a block of wood for doing flat surfaces, or around a dowel, finger, pencil, or file for carved surfaces. Dust the project thoroughly before applying any finish.

Wood Penetrating Oils — Rubbed Finish

Modern wood oils are easy to apply and are actually better than the old-fashioned linseed-oil method, because they have polymerizing agents that seal the wood and retard the darkening to which oiled pieces are prone. Usually you brush it on, let is penetrate, and wipe off the excess. It's quick, and the cleanup is simple. Watco and Minwax make some excellent oils. Watco is harder to find than Minwax, though many woodworkers use it exclusively.

Paint

A few things that can make the difference between a good and a bad paint job are proper surface preparation, brushes, paint, and patience. If you are painting over old enamel (glossy) paint, sand the gloss off or the new paint will peel within a year or so.

Paint stores sell different brushes for latex than for oil-base paints, and many sizes and shapes of each for various purposes. Use a brush of an appropriate size for what you're painting (too small will take forever, too large will be messy). A good quality brush will make painting easier, especially where you need clean edges — around trim, for example. Most people don't take care of their brushes, but a well-cared-for brush will last years. My father still has the brushes he had when I was a kid. He cleans brushes used for oil-base paint first with thinner, then with strong detergent and *hot* water, followed by a hot rinse. He dries the brush carefully with a rag between the thinner and detergent, and after the hot-water rinse. In spite of the advertising for latex, I still use oil-base enamel whenever I paint wood. Latex is fine for plaster, though. I also spend a little extra for better quality paint. It makes the job easier because it flows on and covers better.

Polyurethane and Varnish

Both of these are clear finishes and each can be substituted for the other. Polyurethane is a plastic material and gives surfaces a plastic appearance, but there is no harder and more durable surface for floors. If you don't mind the plastic look, it is a little easier and quicker to get a smooth finish than with varnish. Varnish is an older material, and it looks more natural than the urethane. That's why I prefer it to urethane and use it on wainscoting, shelves, unpainted window frames, and any other project made from a softwood. Note that you should use a brush meant for varnish.

Burning

This is a technique with which I am less familiar, but I hear it is used extensively on the West Coast. All you need is a propane torch and a brush to remove the char. The effect varies with the wood. If you want to try it, test it on a piece of scrap first. The burning actually seals and preserves the wood.

Heights for Chairs, Tables, Work Surfaces, Storage

The sketches show dimensions that are currently considered appropriate. Each dimension line in the sketches

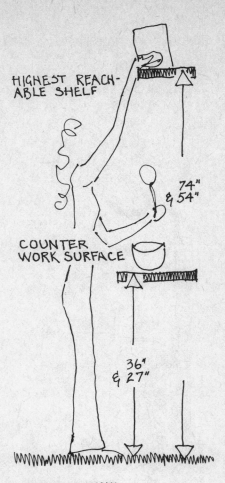

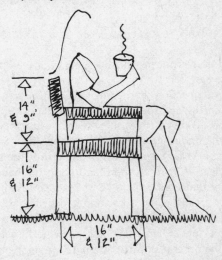

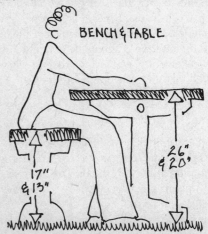

has two numbers by it, corresponding to the standard adult and child. These dimensions may not be exactly correct for everyone. If you are tall or short, you may want to adjust them accordingly. In the case of table height, you may notice it is four inches lower than most tables you buy in furniture stores. Many people agree that 26 inches is a better height than 30 inches.

Each time you build a project, check to be sure your dimensions are appropriate for the purpose they are to serve. If you're building shelves, are the spacings correct for what will occupy them? How big are the books, records, canisters, packages, bottles, linens . . . ? Measure these things before you start to build.

Some Reclaimable Materials and How to Redeem Them

Painted or previously finished boards: Pull nails, sand off the old finish.

shelves
broken-up furniture
table leaves
stair treads
flooring

Construction lumber: Pull nails and use the lumber as is, or sand it smooth.

Wood parts: Clean with wire brush, scrub with soap and water, or strip with paint remover.

stair parts — balusters, newel posts, railings
panels
ornaments — porch balls, roof brackets, moldings
windows
doors
wainscoat
drawers

Other parts:
stained and leaded glass
cast-iron shelf-support brackets
metal fences and gratings

Shopping Hints

Knowing where to get supplies is an important part of any project. There are places to buy new supplies, places to buy used supplies, and places to *find* supplies. As with any other kind of shopping, only practice and experience will yield a catalog of places and develop confidence in your own ability to get what you need.

New materials may be purchased at hardware stores, department stores, conventional lumber yards, and do-it-yourself (consumer-oriented) lumber yards. Used and salvaged materials may be bought at junk yards, lumber salvage yards, flea markets, auctions, second-hand stores, and yard sales. The Yellow Pages are an important source for locating many of these places.

Scavenging requires more ingenuity. You may find materials on the street on garbage day. Look in cellars, garages, and attics. Useful things are found at construction sites (oft called "midnight sales" — or you can ask for cast-aside waste during the day), in houses that are being torn down or have been abandoned, and among debris on the beach. . . .

People who work in hardware stores are generally knowledgeable and are often interested in helping shoppers, especially their regulars. They will answer questions and suggest solutions to problems. In a way, they can be family architects. However, there are at least as many who are not interested in you at all. Many people recalling bad experiences in hardware stores hesitate to shop there. It is worth it to shop around for a genial hardware store and a salesperson who can be a friend and advisor. You pay a little more in a hardware store and should expect better quality and service.

Department stores have some advantages over hardware stores. Tools are often of comparable quality at lower cost. Browsing is more convenient and what items they have are easily found. However, the salespeople are usually less knowledgeable than those in good hardware stores. Many people agree that Sears is the best department store for hardware and tools. Sears' Craftsman tools come with a lifetime guarantee. Other department stores may have lower prices, but their quality is questionable. You can't even trust the old traditional brand names anymore. Most of them produce *throw-away* tools for the consumer market. Remember that a cheaper item may not *be* cheaper if it has to be replaced continually. You can resell or pass a good tool along to a friend, but all you can do with junk is throw it away.

Many lumber yards prefer dealing with the pros, and the salespeople often have little patience with nonprofessional customers. Knowing the lingo will help the casual shopper. Another thought is to look at what they sell. Compare quality, prices, and salespeople in a few yards. This is another place where it helps to develop a friendship with someone who is willing to spend a little time answering questions. There are also those places that cater to the "handyman," the consumer-oriented lumber outlets. They have names like Plywood Palace, Lumber World, U Do It. Some of these are actually excellent sources and others are a rip-off. Check them out.

The salvage yards and second-hand-type stores are places to explore. Things won't be in pretty packages. They may be heaped in piles, or covered with dirt or layers of peeling paint. Imagination is your best companion when visiting these places. Old things are marked with the histories of their owners; but if well-built, they are as good as the day they were new. The well-built junk will be mixed with the real junk. It may take practice and a sharp eye to learn to pick the good from the bad. These kinds of places are found in most communities. Shopping at them can be a pleasant excursion, especially if you find one that you like to visit. If you get to know the salespeople, they will often set aside things that you are looking for, and even phone you when the items appear in the yard or store.

Salvage shopping is growing in popularity. So is scavenging, and it should not be frowned at. Much that appears to be rubbish is not really rubbish at all. It's a matter of developing the nerve and self-confidence to pick up from the ground that which someone else has cast aside. An observant person can collect most of the materials he or she needs without cost.

Boston Area

Blotner Woodcraft Co., 599 Canal St., Lawrence, MA 682-9412.

Building 19 and 19-3/4, 349 Lincoln, Hingham, MA 749-6900.

Central Bldg. & Wrecking Co., 141 Boston St., Everett, MA 387-3700.

Duane's, 600 Southern Artery, Quincy, MA 773-6030.

From Old Mansions, 487 Norfolk, Mattapan, MA 296-0737.

Hercules Building and Wrecking Co., 117 Florence, Brockton, MA 588-3390.

Kouns & Clifford, 14 Norfolk Ave., Roxbury, MA 442-7030.

Materials Recycling Inc., 70 E. Battles, Brockton, MA 843-1575.

Ups & Downs Wrecking Corp., 606 Columbia St., Braintree, MA 848-6000.

Young Engineering and Sales Co., Salem, MA 744-6457.

Cleveland

B and B Wrecking and Excavating, Inc., 5801 Train 651-9090.

Boyas Excavating, Inc., 4100 Brook Park 398-3900.

Broadway Wrecking Co., 3950 E. 86 271-3939.

Elie Lumber and Salvage Co., 2775 E. 71 Pl. 431-8850.

The Harris Wrecking Co., 1963 W. 3rd. 241-1907.

Chicago

Brock Lumber Co., 1250 W. Lake 733-1025.

Colonial Brick Co., 3334 W. Cermak 762-4215.

Cleveland Wrecking Co., 3801 N. Milwaukee Ave., 685-1100.

Daniels Wrecking Co., 1150 W. 119 264-6606.

Illinois Wrecking Co., 3136 W. Taylor 243-8204.

RIP Wrecking Co., 217 N. Kilpatrick 379-9880.

D.C. — Baltimore Area

D.C.

Builders' Miscellaneous Sales Co., 8211 Lee Hwy., Merrifield 560-2888.

General Wrecking Co., 1017 Brentwood Rd. N.E. 529-8177.

Suburban Maryland

Federal Wrecking Co. Inc., 6701 Eads St., Seat Pleasant, MD 336-2800.

Laurel Wrecking Co., MD Route 198, Laurel 725-8991.

Baltimore

Baltimore Salvage Depot, Pratt St., Baltimore. City-operated warehouse for salvageable goods when city knocks down buildings. Occupies three adjacent row houses. Especially good for woodwork (bannisters, moldings, treads, etc.). Open only on Saturdays, 10 a.m. to 2 p.m. *Cash* only.

General Wrecking Co., 300 Old Ordnance Rd. 789-6300.

Larkin Roland Inc., 4300 Barrington Rd. 247-4477.

People doing homesteading (which is very chic in Baltimore) are "modernizing" old houses and throwing away a lot of good stuff. All sorts of goodies.

State Wrecking Co. of Maryland, Inc., 3005 Washington Blvd. 644-2315.

Fort Worth — Dallas

Clanton's Awning Co., 3111 N. Fitzburgh St., Dallas. Beautiful canvas — all colors and textures.

First Monday Sales — last weekend each month, rummage sales. Everything from livestock to tools to clothes to building materials.

Interstate Wrecking Co., 3011 S. Lamar, Dallas. Dimensional wood, structural steel, brick, piping, plumbing fixtures. Four acres.

Miller Wrecking and Excavating Co., 2806 N. Commerce, Ft. Worth. Same stock as Interstate — twelve acres.

Olshan Demolishing Co., 9777 Harry Hines Rd., Dallas. Everything.

Orr-Reed, 1903 Rock Island, Dallas. Salvage yard. Everything. Five acres.

U.S. Government Surplus Depot, Ft. Worth. Tanks, machinery, wire, hose, camping equipment, etc.

Los Angeles Area

Ace Freight Salvage and Building Materials, 4942 Lincoln Cyp. 995-3581.

Big Ten, 787 W. Woodbury Rd., Altadena 681-7434.

Builders Surplus, 2500 S. Main 546-1032.

Cleveland Wrecking Co., 3170 E. Washington Blvd., L.A. 269-0633.

L.A. Wrecking Co., 810 E. 9th 623-3646.

Mead House Wrecking Co., 2895 Sierra Grande 796-4051.

Mox Lumber Co., 307 E. Jefferson 231-2101.

National House Wrecking and Salvage Co., 14519 S. Avalon 321-3867.

Samson Contracting Inc., 4252 Whittier 266-3010.

Viking Land Clearing, 3029 Fierro 254-6741.

Williams Wrecking and Demolition, 1124 Boyle Ave. 255-1675.

Milwaukee

Beallary Bros. Contractors Inc., 14840 Tulane 784-1189.

Beno's Salvage & Supply Co., 11000 W. St. Martins Rd. 354-3444.

Gerovac Wrecking Corp., 11836 W. St. Martins Rd. 425-1500.

Grams Wrecking and Lumber Co., 5050 S. Nicholson 483-5050.

Northwestern Lumber & Wrecking Co., 627 S. 1st 276-1318.

Stein D. and Sons, 1426 S. 21st St., 383-0083, 425-3871.

Wisconsin Wrecking Co., 9144 W. St. Martins Rd. 425-4450.

Barrett Wrecking Inc., 21001 W. Coffee Rd., New Berlin 547-0431.

New York Area

CB Caputo Wrecking and Lumber Inc., 115-01 New York Blvd., Jamaica 658-0578.

Ready Wrecking, 133-40 7602 Pk., Queens 296-8662.

Underwriters Salvage Co. of New York, NYC 748-5450.

Younge Contractor Corp., 2501 Third Ave., NYC. They do demolition. If you ask nicely, it is possible to get stuff — construction lumber, wainscoting — for free. They also sell some stuff. Go to job site they are working on.

Brooklyn

Bilicki Contracting Corp., 142 Grand 384-3840.

Downem Wrecking Co. Inc., 92 Howard Ave. 452-6187.

Fine M. Lumber Co., 175 Varick Ave. 381-5200.

Grossman M. Lumber Corp., 1901 Ralph Ave. 251-1020.

JSJ Wrecking Co., 2291 Pitkin Ave. 235-3576.

Newark and Elizabeth N.J.

Cliffwood Lumber and Wrecking Co., State Hwy. 35, Cliffwood 566-1743.

Igoe Bros., 234 Pioneer St., Newark, NJ 243-3450. Sono-tubes (paper tubes), 12- to 48-inch diameters. Useful for bookcases, planters, shelves.

Jefferson Wreckers Inc., 312 South St., Newark 334-8088 or 351-8917.

Luria Bros. and Co., Inc., 1001 Newark Ave., Elizabeth, NJ 624-4688. Industrial furnaces, machinery supplies, electronic test equipment, lab equipment, office furniture, drafting tables, and other surplus.

Second Avenue Flea Market, Flemington, NJ. Miscellaneous antiques.

Vigilante Wrecking Co. Inc., 725 Riverside Ave., Lyndhurst 939-3014.

New Haven and Stamford Conn.

Allstate Contracting Corp., 12 Hemingway Ave., East Hartford 777-3333.

Stamford Wrecking Co., 330 Fairfield Ave., Stamford, CT 324-9537.

Oregon

Eugene Planing Mill. Source for renovation supplies. List prices. Do custom work also at fairly reasonable prices.

The Horse Trader, Dundee, OR. Very small side of small. Surplus goods and used goods — nails, tools, paints.

Jerry's Building Materials, 2400 99 N., Eugene, OR. 689-1911. Standard building material place, frequented often by architecture students. You have to get there when a shipment comes in, 'cause the good stuff goes fast.

Jim's Trading Post, Grand Ronde, OR. Worth going out of your way to visit. Doesn't often carry used lumber but does periodically have windows, auction-bought building supplies, salvaged plumbing fixtures, and a used book dept. Very inexpensive.

L & L Building Supply, 195 Birds Eye Ave., Woodburn, OR 981-4041. Less expensive building blocks than other places. Occasionally have materials like 1 x 8 and 2 x 4 redwood at low prices.

Ted and Leo Muller Lumber, 5 miles west of Salem on Salem Independence Road. 364-0523. Honest people. Some of the lowest prices around. Stock from bankruptcy sales, mill sales, and auctions — varies from day to day. Economy and standard grade lumbers.

Recycled Lumber, Rt. 99 W., Rickreall, OR. 623-3603. Small side of small. Almost entirely salvaged goods. Reasonable prices. Good place to look just in case.

E. S. Ritter, Inc., 4952 Portland Rd. N.E., Salem, OR. 393-7101. Good place for recycled goods. But prices are just a little high. Stock varies. You haul your own and bring your own saw.

West 11th Salvage Yard, Eugene, OR. Small — entirely used goods, especially windows and some plumbing. Sometimes have leaded glass windows.

Whole Earth Pump and Hardware, Grand Ronde, OR. Good supply of used tools, do-it-yourself books, plumbing and basic hardware.

Philadelphia Area

Bankrupt Stock by Thomas E. Stetson, Buyers and Sellers of General Merchandise, 4954 Old York Rd., Philadelphia, PA 455-4333.

Cleveland Wrecking Co., 702 Chester Pk., Sharon Hill 729-2700.

Ferro's Used Brick Dealer, 7245 Grays Ave., Philadelphia, PA 727-1351.

Franklin Electric Co., Surplus Electric Supplies, 1511 N. 26th St., Philadelphia, PA 765-3965.

Mack Frazier, 1909 N. Ringgold St., Philadelphia, PA 763-5057. Used building materials.

Mittin Bros. Inc., Wolf and Swanson, Philadelphia, PA 368-8500.

Wilmington, Del.

Diamond State Terminal Co., Ft. of Christians Ave., 726-0939.
George Wilson Wrecking Co., 403 N. Dupont 658-7165.
Wrights Service Co., 433 Newcastle Ave. 654-5326.

St. Louis

Aalco Wrecking Co. Inc., 901 S. 14 231-3255.
Bicunas Bldg. Products, 3500 Chouto 664-2422
Binder & Son Lumber & Bldg. Supply, Hwy. 40 at K 441-1224.
Gaines Bros., 3823 Washington Ave. 371-2770.
Poor Boy Jim's Wrecking Co., 5440 Martin Luther King 522-1450.
Beyers Lumber Co., 8684 Olive St. Rd. 993-2445.
Hayden Lumber & Wrecking Co., 999 N. 40, E. St. Louis 271-2013.

St. Paul & Minneapolis Area

All State Salvage Inc., 1354 Jackson, St. Paul 488-6675. Building material, plumbing, furniture.
Bauer Bros. Salvage, 174 Arlington Ave. E. 489-9044.
The Great Minneapolis Surplus Store — Eastgate Store: 309 Central Ave. N.E. 338-2920. Robbinsdale Store: 4066 Hwy. 52 537-1637. Genuine U.S. Surplus.

San Francisco Bay Area

Allen Abdo Salvage Co., 718 Douglas Ave., Oakland 569-2070.
Arons Building Wrecking Co., 4245 W. Capitol Ave., W. Sacramento 371-5473.
Bayview Lumber, 336 Adeline, Oakland 836-3392.
Bay-Wide Destruction Co., 681 Market St., San Francisco 495-4272.
Brothers Used Lumber, Treasure Is. Rd., Yrba Bnd Is. 982-1484.
Caldwell Building Wreckers 756-3276.
Charles S. Campanella Building Materials, 2700 E. 7th 536-7002.
Harvest Materials, P.O. Box 24411 921-4949.
Jennings Salvage, 1133 Ohio Ave., Richmond 232-5843.
Oakland Building Materials Co., 1224 22nd Ave., Oakland 532-7116.
Ralphs Bill, 29 Berry, San Francisco 957-1174.
Sunrise Salvage, 2210 San Pablo Ave., Berkeley 845-4751.
Zamora House Wrecking Co., 2932 E. 7th, Oakland 533-5737.

Headings to Explore in the Yellow Pages

General

Building materials, used
Furniture dealers, used

Junk dealers
Lumber, used
Second-hand dealers
Surplus merchandise
Thrift shops
Wrecking contractors

Specific

Awnings
Boxes
Brick
Builders' hardware
Canvas products
Cardboard
Clay products
Coated fabrics
Concrete products
Contractors, tile
Cork
Cork insulation
Cotton
Doors
Electric supplies
Floor materials
Glass, stained and leaded
Granite
Greenhouse
Hardboard
Hardware
Hides
Hinges
Kettles
Lampshades
Leather
Lighting
Linoleum
Mailboxes
Marble
Mats and matting
Millwork
Mirrors
Mosaics
Packing and crating
Paper tubes and cores
Pipe, used
Planter boxes
Plastics
Plumbing fixtures and supplies, used
Plywood
Quilts
Rattan
Refinishing, baked enamel
Rock
Rope
Rubber, foam and sponge
Shelving

Shutters
Slate
Stone
Tanners
Tiles
Timber connectors
Wallboard
Wall covering
Windowshades
Wood turning
Woodworking supplies